ALSO BY ANTWONE FISHER

Finding Fish: A Memoir

Who Will Cry for the Little Boy?: Poems

A BOY SHOULD KNOW

HOW TO TIE A TIE

AND
OTHER LESSONS
FOR
SUCCEEDING IN LIFE

ANTWONE FISHER

A TOUCHSTONE BOOK
Published by Simon & Schuster
NEW YORK   LONDON   TORONTO   SYDNEY

Touchstone
A Division of Simon & Schuster, Inc.
1230 Avenue of the Americas
New York, NY 10020

First Touchstone hardcover edition April 2010

TOUCHSTONE and colophon are registered trademarks of
Simon & Schuster, Inc.

For information about special discounts for bulk purchases,
please contact Simon & Schuster Special Sales at 1-800-506-1949
or business@simonandschuster.com.

The Simon & Schuster Speakers Bureau can bring authors to your live
event. For more information or to book an event contact the
Simon & Schuster Speakers Bureau at 1-866-248-3049 or visit our
website at www.simonspeakers.com.

Designed by Joy O'Meara
Illustrations by John Del Gaizo

Manufactured in the United States of America

10   9   8   7   6   5   4   3   2   1

Library of Congress Cataloging-in-Publication Data
Fisher, Antwone Quenton.
A boy should know how to tie a tie : and other lessons for succeeding in
life / by Antwone Fisher.—1st Touchstone hbk. ed.
      p. cm.
1. Young men—Conduct of life. 2. Young men—Life skills guide.
I. Title.
BJ1671.F57 2009
646.7—dc22
2009053235

ISBN 978-1-4165-6662-5
ISBN 978-1-4165-6685-4 (ebook)

For Fletcher Keith Burkley

A gentleman of the first class and always remembered

A LETTER TO MY YOUNGER SELF

Dear Antwone,

I know that you don't have much in the way of material things, more importantly a father to teach you those important things that a boy will need to learn on his journey to manhood. Like you, my beginnings were unremarkable, and I do understand your curiosity, confusion, and your feelings of uncertainty about your future.

True, you were born without parents and a loving home to call your own, but you have everything you need inside of you to create a wonderful successful life for yourself, so you have to begin with you, by preparing yourself for that remarkable future.

I've written this book you hold in your hands from the lessons that I've learned while on the journey to manhood and success, to be used as a guide or reference tool for you, and boys such as you, to use as you make your way to manhood and beyond. I'm confident that with this guide, a wonderful life of dreams beyond your dreams come true awaits you.

Warmly,
Your future self,
Antwone

CONTENTS

INTRODUCTION

All right now, men, listen and listen close. Some of you may think you know how to perform this simple task. I'm here to tell you that you don't know a thing until the navy tells you you know it."

My company commander, a tall, reedlike man with a chin like the bow of ship and a prominent Adam's apple that bobbed up and down like a life boat, fixed his eyes on each of the sixty recruits in formation in front of him. I stood as tall as I could, eyes forward, a length of black cloth snaking from my hand. When I sensed the company commander wasn't looking my way, I nervously ran my tongue around the perimeter of my upper lip, checking for perspiration. Finding none, I was glad that my body wasn't betraying my mind and spirit. I was not ready for this.

In the first few weeks since I'd entered the Great Lakes Naval Recruit Training Center in suburban Chicago, I'd endured many things. Whether it was the brutal physical training, the endless hours of classroom work, or the hours of instruction regarding every aspect of how to conduct myself, dress, and march, I hadn't anticipated this horror.

As I stood there, I remembered that night two days before Christmas when I stepped off the bus and into the frigid air of an Illinois winter and experienced a similar chill. Now the company commander held in front of him, extended between his spread fingers, a strip of fabric identical to the one I held in my own moist hands.

"This is the half-Windsor knot. You will at all times and without exception tie your tie in this fashion." With a series of deft moves, the straight length of cloth was twisted and turned into a neat and orderly bit of neckwear. In my imagination he was like Charlton Heston in *The Ten Commandments*, standing in front of a group of nonbelievers as he transformed a staff into a snake. Though none of us fell on bended knee to ask for forgiveness, all the same, *How did he do that?* was on many of our minds.

After he completed his demonstration, the company commander announced that he would give us all a minute to practice what he'd just demonstrated. At the end of that minute, we'd all be required to undo our knot and wait for our turn to step in front of him and demonstrate our mastery of the technique. My inept fingers felt like sausages as I fumbled with the wooly serpent. I shook my head in exasperation and shut my eyes in frustration. I'd tried to pay attention to what he was doing, but though my ears had heard and my mind had registered the technique, I could not produce the same knot as my company commander. I tore my mangled mess apart in frustration, exhaled to try to relax the tense muscles in my face and neck. I stood awaiting my fate.

Whether it was going to be Military Training Unit—extra training during which I would have to run through an obstacle course set up in the enormous drill hall—or something worse, failing this task meant the risk of being held back an additional week in my training. I wanted neither of those things to happen. But what choice did I have? I'd never learned to tie a tie before, and one quick demonstration wasn't going to overcome those years I'd spent in ignorance.

Unfortunately, I was in the middle of the pack of recruits, so I had to spend an agonizing few minutes waiting for my humiliation to begin. I heard a few of the recruits being dismissed after successfully copying the company commander's taut knot, and a few others being told, "No good. Again." I watched as the failures walked past me to the end of the line, their eyes downcast, their expressions either sullen or incredulous.

My mind drifted back to my days in Cleveland when I lived in foster care. The man with whom I lived, a Pentecostal minister by the name of Reverend Pickett, had a rigid routine when he returned from his day job as a landscaper. He would come home in his matching khaki shirt and pants—the uniform he chose to wear for his entrepreneurial landscaping business. Depending upon the season, his shirt might be darkened by crescent moons of perspiration underneath his arms or an island of brown between his shoulder blades. In almost every season and on almost every day, there'd be a faint impression of dirt amid the rippled folds on the knees of his trousers.

Reverend Pickett would go into his room and later emerge from his early-evening shower dressed in a pair of neatly pressed slacks and a crisp white dress shirt. The woodsy smell of his aftershave trailed behind him as he made his way to a mirror in the hallway. There he'd carefully fold his suit coat over a nearby chair and stand regarding his reflection, tilting his head at various angles like a vigilant dog. Next he'd carefully brush his hair around the sides and to the back of his balding head. Then, like a magician, he'd tie his necktie with a precision and flair that mesmerized me. He'd be sure that the tip of the tie was even with his belt buckle, and then shrug his way into his suit coat and pull down on the lapels like he was cinching the straps of a parachute. As a final touch, he tucked a pocket square into the jacket's breast pocket and clapped his hands. He'd leave the house to go off and do battle with the devil.

His transformation enthralled me. It seemed to me that his necktie was the source of his prominence in the community and exuded the sense of command and control that even as a preteen I so longed for. Someday, I told myself, I'd wear a suit and tie and people would think of me as strong and admirable. It would take many years and a young lifetime full of trials and tribulations—days spent wondering where my next meal was going to come from or where I was going to sleep for the night—before any thoughts beyond the immediate future could penetrate the fog I lived in. Joining the navy was a way out of that fog, but I was still looking days and weeks ahead, not years.

If I made it through the navy's basic training, I knew I'd be rewarded with, among other things, a naval dress blue uniform. At the time, enlisted men were issued black shoes, black slacks, a white shirt, a double-breasted black suit jacket in the admiral style with six silver buttons, and a black tie. All would have to be worn according to navy regulations. As I stood in line about to face our company commander, in my mind's eye, I saw that suit receding farther and farther into the darkness. If I couldn't tie a tie correctly, I felt like I'd never graduate and take my place with the rest of the company. I'd end up back in Cleveland, rootless and restless, struggling to find my place in the world—a world that seemed determined to squash any of my aspirations.

The company commander's expression of disapproval told me all I needed to know. I swallowed a throat-tightening bit of disappointment and made my way to the back of the line, avoiding eye contact with the rest of the recruits. *Why hadn't my foster father taught me to tie a damned tie* was all I could think in that moment. Didn't he know that it was one of the most basic skills a young man would need if he was going to improve his lot in life? Of course, my foster parents didn't teach me a lot of things, and the things the Reverend and his wife did drill into me mostly consisted of lectures about my being a no-account, ungrateful boy. At times they wanted to tie me up and whip me, but they weren't about to teach me to tie a necktie. After all, I was never—according to them—going to take a place in society where I would need to be dressed appropriately, unless it was at my trial for crimes yet to be committed. I guess they figured it was up to my lawyers to determine how to make me as presentable as possible to a jury.

Little did they know that the only jury I would ever face consisted of my superiors in the U.S. Navy and in particular a hard-ass company commander who was separating the wheat from the chaff with clocklike regularity. "You're good." "You're not." Either judgment was rendered with the same impassive tone, indicating neither congratulations nor disappointment. As the minutes went by and we were given further demonstrations, the wheat field was harvested until only a couple of stalks remained. Finally, it was just me and the harvester, and images of him as Death with his hooded eyes and his crescent-shaped scythe replaced the squared-away officer in my imagination. In the fluorescent light, his pallid skin lent an even more cadaverous element to his demeanor.

In reality, his expression softened and his bark was replaced with a calm and measured tone. He stood directly in front of me, his eyes intently focused only on me.

"Recruit Fisher, you *will* do this. I will not let you fail. You will not let yourself fail."

He undid the haphazard half done knot I'd been struggling with. Draping the tie around my neck, he began his litany of instructions and demonstrated the procedure for me: "First, the wide end W should extend approximately twelve inches past narrow end N."

He did as instructed.

"Cross the wide end W over the narrow end N. Then bring the wide end W around and behind the narrow end N."

Again, he performed the actions as he described. His face remained impassive. It was almost as if I was in an episode of the old TV show *Mission Impossible* and I was Mr. Phelps listening to the tape recording. The difference was, I had no choice but to accept this mission.

"Next, bring the wide end W up and pull it through the loop formed by the intersecting ends. Bring the wide end in front, over the narrow end from right to left. Stay with me. Now, again, bring the wide end *W* up and through the loop."

I exhaled for what seemed to be the first time since we had started this one-on-one lesson.

"Bring the wide end *W* down through the knot in front. Finally, using both hands, tighten the knot carefully and draw it up to your collar."

I had to fight a smile from spreading across my lips. The company commander looked at me and nodded. Then he reached out for me and cinched the knot a little more, "Nice and tight. So you won't forget you've got one on. Or how it got there."

HOW TO TIE A TIE

He told me to go to the head (a military term for bathroom) and practice doing it on my own. I wish I could say that my fingers no longer felt like sausages and my brain was no longer a runny bowl of oatmeal, but I still could not get it right. I stood looking in that mirror, cursing Reverend Pickett who seemed to have kept his magician's secret from me for so long that even the navy's vast experience in instructing recruits could not undo my ignorance. That anger and frustration hampered me in my efforts to concentrate. I kept thinking of my fellow recruits, spending their little bit of idle relaxation while I was in the head watching a mirror image of myself screw up. I didn't like the man I saw in the glass in front of me.

Eventually, through perseverance, I did learn to tie a half-Windsor knot that day. I did go on to graduate from basic training and I served eleven years in the navy, traveling the world and experiencing things a poor and fatherless young man from Cleveland couldn't have imagined. Years later after I'd left the navy, I had other occasions to bump up against the painful realization that a boy ought to know how to tie a tie. One such occasion occurred when I was privileged to attend an awards ceremony. Being there on one of Hollywood's most glamorous nights was a source of enormous pride. As the houselights dimmed, I thought of my foster father again because I had once again been confronted by my ignorance when faced with the prospect of tying a bow tie for this formal event. And again for my wedding a few years later, I had selected a ruffled shirt with a bow tie paired with a morning suit. I had stood there debating whether to settle for something less than what I wanted, knowing that a bow tie was still beyond my range of skills, but I refused to settle. The sales clerk who sold me the outfit was happy to instruct me.

Gratefully, no thoughts of my foster mother and foster father intruded on the glorious day when I married my bride, LaNette. I had put behind me many of the thoughts of my emotionally impoverished childhood in the foster care system, the brief but frightening period I spent homeless, and the gaping hole in my life that my parents' absence had torn in my world. It wasn't as if I'd completely forgotten all of those painful events that had marked and marred my early years. I'd transformed those experiences into a best-selling memoir entitled *Finding Fish*. The critically acclaimed film was called *Antwone Fisher* and, amazingly, it was directed by Denzel Washington, one of the most respected men in Hollywood. I'd gone from the backlots of Hollywood studios where I worked as a security guard (after a stint as a prison guard) to the executive suites where I pitched my screenplays. Working through my feelings of abandonment and abuse had been difficult but beneficial.

As a consequence of the book and film about my life, I received thousands of messages of congratulations and an equal number of questions about how I was able to make the transformation I did. To be honest, I appreciated the acclaim but wasn't always certain I was capable of responding to the queries. How I did it seemed as mystifying to me as how to tie a tie had been in my early naval career. I knew that my military experience had transformed me, but I wasn't so sure how I'd managed to have the sense to grab the lifeline that was offered to me. Unlike many in Hollywood who dabble in various spiritual and religious matters, I'm not an active seeker of wisdom from various traditions. Once I was sitting in a production company's waiting room before a meeting, and I was flipping through a magazine. I came across this Buddhist expression in *Tricycle* magazine, "What lies behind you, and what lies before you, is nothing compared to what lies within you."

I know that it's easy to offer up ancient wisdom as the answer to life's difficult questions. That doesn't make it any easier to polish a shoe, balance a checkbook, fix a healthy dinner, or decide whether or not an extended warranty on a new flat-screen TV is worth the cost. (It's not.) We all face daily questions that push those more important philosophical issues into the background. That said, I do believe that what lies within all of us is the answer to the question so often posed to me about how I managed to "make it" in this world.

The book you hold in your hands is part instruction manual, part guidebook, and part reflection. As a younger man, I spent all those hours in front of a mirror trying to learn to tie a tie. Now that I'm a lot older, I've held the mirror up to myself again so that I can offer guidance to those of you who, like me, have had questions that no one in your life seems willing or able to answer. I'll address matters of fashion and grooming, conduct and planning, using examples from my own life to illustrate both the how and the why. I don't consider myself an expert; I'm just someone who has lived a life and gathered experiences. As a writer, it is my nature and my gift to be an observer. From my earliest days as a child I frequently stood apart and watched—sometimes forced to and other times by choice—as humanity went about its business. I've traveled great distances geographically, emotionally, and experientially, and like a photographer taking a step back to better frame his subject, I've taken the time to distance myself from all that has happened and all the choices that I've made that have led me to this happy and content place in my life.

Though as I was going through my life I can't say that I had a five-year, ten-year, or even a single-year plan for myself that I laid out on paper, I did have a vision of who I wanted to be firmly set in my mind. It took years for that vision to be realized, but in looking back I can see that what I had inside me enabled me to make that vision come to life. Just as a movie is a collaborative effort, I have many people to thank for assisting me with this production. I hope that I can offer you the kind of guidance and support that I received from valued contributors along the way. One thing I've learned in my years in Hollywood is that no matter how good the script I write, someone else will have ideas that will strengthen it, open up new possibilities, directions, and insights. I'm offering you my advice, but you have to bring your own sensibility to the project of creating your own life. Please don't think of what I have to say as a template you can trace; instead, think of my words as a starting point for your own exploration. It's never too late, or too soon, to get going, so let's begin.

CHAPTER ONE

KEEPING YOURSELF VALUABLE

In some ways, growing up as a foster child in Cleveland, Ohio, in the 1960s, I had one advantage over other kids in my neighborhood. I knew what my value was. That value began as the $2.20 a day the great state of Ohio, the Buckeye State, paid to a woman by the name of Mrs. Strange, who was my first foster care mother. That money covered the expenses for my board and food. Of course, the money meant nothing to me when I was an infant.

It took some investigation to discover that little tidbit while I was writing *Finding Fish*. Mrs. Strange doesn't figure very prominently in that account of my life. Mizz Pickett and the Reverend Pickett, the older black couple who took me in at the age of two, do figure prominently, and they made me almost painfully aware of my value to them. Mizz Pickett frequently referred to the underage mother who had abandoned me to the state's child welfare services as my "no-account mammy." In my ignorance, I interpreted that expression literally; my mother was too poor to have a bank account. I wasn't far off. The expression no-account means "worthless."

And, despite the constant reminders from Mizz Pickett that she took in her other foster children and me so that she could "pay her notes" or bills (which made no sense to me at the time) and that she could take me back to where she got me, I was aware that I had some monetary value to her. Otherwise, the theme of her many speeches seemed to be, *Why else would she keep me around?* I never really knew the exact dollar amount she was paid for fostering Flo, Dwight, and me, but apparently in her mind it wasn't enough. She filched the five-dollar allowance the state provided for me. It seemed to me when I discovered the fact I had an allowance at all, that I was worth a lot more than the Picketts seemed to think.

I've introduced Mrs. Strange and the Picketts, but let me offer you a brief overview of my life, assuming you are not familiar with its contents. If you have read *Finding Fish*, you will know this story of my early years. My biological mother and father never had a chance to get married, and it's unlikely that they ever would have. While my mother was still carrying me in her womb, my father, Edward (Eddie) Elkins, was killed by a shotgun blast. He was involved in a heated dispute with the mother of his two other children, and he never imagined she would pull the trigger. But she did, killing him almost instantly. My mother was incarcerated when I was born, and I was placed into the foster care system from infancy.

After Mrs. Strange, I spent many unhappy years with the Picketts, where I was subjected to emotional and physical abuse. I shared this unhappiness with two other foster children there—Flo and Dwight—and together we could see the Picketts' own children treated in a much better fashion. I was sexually abused over the course of many years by a woman who was one of the Picketts' neighbors and who was tasked with looking after me on one of the many occasions when Mizz Pickett was not at home. Of course, Mizz Pickett never projected her true self out to the world, and while caseworkers did check on me over the years, none of them knew the true extent of what I suffered. Along with the physical abuse came a never-ending stream of discouraging words and negativity, the kind of soul-crushing cruelty a young boy can barely survive. But for many years, I knew no better.

My treatment at the hands of the Reverend and Mizz Pickett grew increasingly worse over the years. For a while, I viewed Mr. Pickett as a kindly but removed father figure in my life. But I was shocked one day when I realized that, after many years under his roof, he didn't even know my name. As the Picketts withdrew more and more, their house became overrun by strangers and as a boy I was left to fend for myself. After the book *Finding Fish,* I published a collection of poetry entitled *Who Will Cry for the Little Boy?*

After my care totally collapsed, I was again in the hands of the state of Ohio. It was only then that I received a gift basket that contained cologne and other things a father might give to his son. When I received these, I was back in the orphanage where my life began.

I then lived through a relatively brief but desperate period of homelessness before I enlisted in the United States Navy and began my slow but steady ascent from lost boyhood to a more fulfilling and fruitful manhood.

We All Live in the Material World

I realize that the majority of you reading this won't be a part of the foster care system, and will come from families that support and nurture you. That doesn't mean that there won't be times when you feel devalued and deprived in ways large and small. It is interesting to be writing about human value at this particular point in history, when we are in the midst of an economic decline that has some comparing it to the Great Depression. While we will eventually find our way out of this "Great Recession," the roots of this hardship can be found in our society's emphasis on the acquisition of objects, whether they are homes or what our stock portfolios can provide for us—clothes, jewelry, automobiles, and the latest high-tech gadgets.

We live at a time when our appetite for material goods is only outweighed by the burdensome debt so many of us carry. It is as if we measure our worth in terms of the square footage of our homes, the number of friends we acquire on Facebook, and the number of gigabytes our iPods, smart phones, and computers can carry. We want more and more and more, and I sometimes think that's because we value ourselves less and less.

Now, of course, I understand that as human beings we are valuable in many ways that can't be measured in dollars and cents. It took some time to come to that realization, particularly because of the emotional and spiritual poverty in which I lived as a child. The Cleveland neighborhood in which I was raised wasn't the finest community in the world, and most of my peers lived under similar financial restraints. As much as I admire that Buddhist statement about what is inside each of us being so important, as a kid, I lived in a world of externals, in the here and now, and in the present. I was constantly being told that even though there was this dollar amount attached to me, I wasn't worth a whole lot to the Picketts. Whether it was having my Halloween candy confiscated and being told that I could have some when I "deserved" it, to watching the Picketts' biological children and their favorite foster child open presents on Christmas morning while the "terrible trio" of Flo, Dwight, and myself stood by empty-handed and heavyhearted, the message was clear: I wasn't worth very much to my foster parents.

I so bought into the notion—and I use that expression purposely—that money spent and dollars collected equaled someone's value, that at one point I stole some pocket change from Mizz Pickett. I was sorely tempted to go to the corner grocer and see a different and better reality through Lemonhead eyes, visit exotic locales through Boston Baked Beans and Charleston Chews, and tempt fate with Jaw Breakers. I didn't. Instead, I took the money and offered it to other kids at school, hoping that I could taste the sweet confection of human connection. Attention and interaction are just other forms of human transactions, items up for sale to the highest bidder if that's the only way you can see it.

As sad as it was that as a young foster child I was forced to view the world that way, I sometimes wonder, when I see how the world operates today, if the difference between my upbringing and my relationship with the concept of value is a matter of degree and not of kind. In other words, I look around, now that I'm living comfortably near Beverly Hills, and I have by all accounts "made it" in this society. I see a world in which most people associate their value with something material—possessions, salary, investment accounts, the kind of car they drive, and everything else that can be assigned a dollar amount. I find it ironic that if you want to know how much money, let's say, your heirloom Piaget watch is worth, you take it to an appraiser. Sounds like someone who is going to praise you for having the good sense, good fortune (another tricky word, that one), or good heritage to have an object like that in your possession.

It's All Relative

That appraiser of fine timekeeping devices will tell you what your watch is worth, but sometimes that dollar amount doesn't jibe with what you think it's worth. What if that Piaget watch is one your great-aunt Carole wore on the day that she was in Washington, D.C., attending President John Fitzgerald Kennedy's inauguration and it had been a gift to her from your great-grandmother upon graduation from Smith College? Or what if it is a plain old Timex your great-aunt Emma wore while taking part in the Birmingham garbage strike with Dr. Martin Luther King, Jr., and that was presented to you upon your graduation from Grambling College?

Who's to say which one has the higher value, which of the two should have its praises sung the loudest and the longest?

We say of those kinds of objects that they have sentimental value, and we can assign sentimental value to anything from the exclusive, like a Piaget watch, to the inexpensive, like the saved stub from the movie ticket you purchased the first time you went to see one of your own screenplays performed in a theater for public consumption. We also attach value to things that are intangible, like the feeling of satisfaction I might take from having crafted a line of dialogue in my latest project. That line could end up being revised, excised, or even vilified by a critic as lame, but given the right attitude, none of that should diminish the value of the sense of pride and pleasure I take in and after the moment of its creation.

Okay, Antwone, you might be thinking, *you're losing me with all this talk about value and dollars. What does that have to do with anything about me?* Well, let me make a few more comments about this general idea of value and making yourself valuable. Who ultimately decides whether or not something has worth? For example, you see an ad on craigslist for a used Fender Highway One Precision bass guitar for $750. The ad goes on to say that it once belonged to Neil Davis who played for a band called Messy Basement. You've never heard of him or his band, but you know the model of the guitar and it's considered a pretty decent instrument. You go to all kinds of pricing guides, check out some auctions on eBay, and you mentally calculate that it is worth $600 at most. You respond to the ad, playing the game of bargaining, and offer $550 for it, figuring you've given yourself some room to negotiate. The owner responds that he can't let it go for anything less than $675. You figure he's come down in asking price by $75, and do some additional calculating to see if you think you can still get him down to your $600 estimated top "worth" figure. You bump your offer up to $575 and hope that he goes for it, or at least gets closer to $600. You don't hear from him for a few days and you figure this is all a part of the game, but finally you lose some of your discipline and e-mail him saying that you'll go to $600. Another day or two passes, and then you get his reply: someone else bought it for his original asking price.

You think, *What? Who in the world would pay $750 for that? The Official Vintage Guitar Price Guide* said it was only worth $575 to $675 depending upon condition. And your Google search of Messy Basement produced only one reference to the musical group, and that was a horrific, out-of-focus video on YouTube of the group's performance in what looked to be their own or perhaps someone else's messy basement. Go figure. (Please note: Don't waste your valuable time doing a Google search for Messy Basement the band. I made that up, but there are a lot of photos on the Internet of people's disorganized basements and cluttered crawl spaces. I won't make any judgment about these people or how they do and don't spend—another one of those money words—their time.)

I hope it's clear what my point is. The value of that guitar was a matter of personal choice. An object that held a certain "objective" value in your mind was of a much higher value in someone else's. The same is true of the value that you place on yourself, on your family members, your friends, and everything and everyone else in your life.

Think about it: how many times in a normal day do you say or think, "That's (not) worth it"? We make value judgments, literally and metaphorically, all the time. But so often, we assign these values based on our perceptions at the moment, and that does not mean that they are always accurate or necessarily astute.

Your Value is Relative

I begin with the tricky nature of value because whenever I'm asked that ubiquitous question: How did you *do* it?, the one answer that keeps popping into my head is that at some point, I figured I was worth it. I figured that I was deserving of that Halloween candy that had been spirited away from me and locked in a box. I found somewhere inside of me a note that said, "You are worth more than that $2.20 a day." I think that note was always there, that even when the world was shouting at me that I was worthless, I could find a lighted place inside me where I could unfold that note and read it to myself. Who put that note there? I sometimes wonder if maybe it was Mrs. Strange, a woman who, by all accounts, showed me great kindness. My caseworker's records indicate that Mrs. Strange had been admonished for holding me too close, that her well-intentioned gesture might have negative consequences: she and I might have developed too close of a bond—another of those interesting money words.

In truth, Mrs. Strange did express some reservations about keeping me around for exactly that reason. She was just supposed to be a temporary shelter from the storm, not some place to be permanently anchored. The prospect of me being adopted or returned to my birth mother figured prominently in the mind of Social Services. As an infant, my chances of the former occurring were far greater than the latter. In one sense, I had more value to prospective adoptive parents as an infant than I would as I got older. Sad to think that my value would diminish as I aged; I was the opposite of a fine cheese or a wine or an heirloom watch. Like beauty, value is in the eyes of the beholder and there will always be competing estimates of that quality.

I don't have the answer to who instilled that sense of my own worthiness inside me. In the end, it doesn't matter to me so much whether it was God or some twist of genetic fiber that formed just so, or if aliens came down and implanted it in me. What counts is that it was there and that I eventually recognized that I had that inherent value and acted on it. In my mind, it doesn't matter that it took a very long time (measured in standards imposed by other people) for the world at large to recognize my value and the contributions I've made. Unlike wine or cheese, we don't have dates by which we are considered at our peak. And I've yet to come across any person who has a freshness date stamped on him or her, a "best if used by" label. Just as we determine what our value is, we make the choices about when—or if—we put that value on display for others. Regardless, we have an intrinsic value; we are valuable just because we are.

You Determine Your Value

I know that other terms for what I'm talking about are "self-worth" and "self-esteem." Psychologists and counselors are fond of those terms, and they frequently apply them to young people and their development. They believe that a lot of the trouble young people get into—drugs, drinking, sexual promiscuity, criminality, and assorted other social ills—springs from a lack of self-esteem. Believe me, I've experienced what the world can do to you and how it can either work to erode whatever self-esteem you have or prevent it from developing in the first place. That's only if you let it. Just as you determine your own value, and just as there is no answer to the mystery of where it originates, only you can diminish your own value, and only you can decide to sell off that part of you.

As you mature, you're going to be subjected to people who will evaluate you and judge you, whether peers, family, or other adults in your community. That's just how it is, and believe it or not, that doesn't change a whole lot as you get older. As an adult, you may not have someone in a position of authority like a teacher who will assign you a letter grade to evaluate your performance at work, or as a partner in a romantic relationship, as a parent, or just generally as a citizen of the planet, but there are folks out there all the time talking about you. "Look at that idiot? Did you see him turn left from the right lane? What a knucklehead." You may not hear judgments like that, but they are being rendered about you.

I work in an industry where failure is the norm and success is the exception. I have no way of knowing how many screenplays are written in any particular year, but the number of them that actually go into production is miniscule in comparison to the prodigious outpouring of screenplays that are never produced. Just as people ask me how I left foster care and survived and endured to become a productive member of society, they also ask me how I manage to stay sane in the crazy world of movie making. Let me tell you, it isn't easy now, and it was a lot harder when I was starting out. But a lot of what I've accomplished has to do with that belief in my own worthiness and ability as a writer. The movie opens on that and the credits roll on that as well.

It definitely helps that I have a couple of films under my belt, but that doesn't mean anyone is going to judge my work with any less scrutiny. If nothing else, the standard rises as you move past your first success. People expect more of you once you are a produced and credited writer. So if you think about how difficult it is to go through life, your early years and beyond, with people judging you, the fact is that we are always being judged. I'm sympathetic, and especially to anyone who is laboring under the kind of burden that I did as a kid, where the most significant people in your life are telling you that you have no value. But you can't let those voices shout down the one in your own heart that's telling you they're wrong, that you *are* worth something. To accept the notion that you are worthless is to cultivate the kind of hopelessness that undermines self-esteem and leads to behavior that is negative, or worse—harmful to yourself or others. Instead of accepting that message myself, I heard that one piercing and heartachingly beautiful voice that came from inside and told me that I was worth something. I listened to that message and I believed it, and doing so has made all the difference.

Finding That Message

So how do you go about conducting your own appraisal so that you can at least begin to hum your own praises until you figure out how to put them into words? The first step is to figure out who you are and what it is you like to do. As I write this, the academic year has just started and my older daughter, Indigo, has just entered a new school. She's in seventh grade, and that's a tough time (as if there ever isn't a tough time) to be the new kid. Her teacher, of course, didn't know all the new students and not all the kids in the class knew one another. So the teacher asked each of the kids to say a little something about themselves by way of introduction. Indigo said that one student stood in silence for a few seconds and then said, "I don't know. I don't know myself. I don't know what to say."

And the teacher said, "That's deep."

As a seventh grader, this poor little thing is only eleven or twelve years old and probably felt like she was put on the spot. I know all about being shy and unwilling to share my thoughts with other people. But I was also thinking that at least by eleven kids should know a little bit about themselves, meaning what they like to do, what they like to eat, if they've traveled any place with their family, if they enjoyed that travel. More important, do they like themselves? And if they do, what about themselves do they like the most? Sometimes those early dreams of being a veterinarian or a painter or an astronaut, while they can seem far out, ultimately find a way to develop, to transform, and a kernel of those early ambitions survives into our adulthood and informs who we become.

Some people enter their teen years and never stop to consider who they are. And I think that before you can see yourself as valuable, you have to explore who you are on the inside. Parents can help their kids do that and certainly play a huge role in any child's development—or lack thereof. Parents should encourage their kids to spend time thinking about who they are by thinking about what they like to do, what their friends are like as people, the qualities they'd like their friends to have. For their part, kids need to be honest with themselves and pay attention to these questions as they become increasingly important. One great way to do this is to take notes—whether that comes in the form of a formal journal or diary (no, diaries are not strictly for girls to write about their crushes or BFFs), or simply keeping track of important thoughts as you have them. Seeing things in writing makes you think about them differently. I'll advocate for you to keep track of your progress in a journal throughout this book, so if you are along for the ride, commit to getting a journal of some kind and reinforcing all of your goals with the written word. Identifying what qualities you have and what skills you have is the first step in calculating your own self-worth. Notice that I didn't say that you should go around and ask other people what *they* think of you; instead, ask yourself what *you* think of you.

Indigo could easily answer the teacher's questions. She knows that she likes to draw, to travel, eat pralines and ice cream, and play soccer. Those things sound simple enough, but I wonder how many of us as kids have thought about it? The harder question, of course, is what do we like *about ourselves*. I recently read about a research study in which kids were asked what they liked about themselves. The results didn't surprise me, but girls most often commented on something about their appearance: their hair, their eyes, and that kind of thing. Boys were different. They most often commented on the things they could do: I'm a good football player; I can jump high. Each kind of answer has its rewards and its challenges.

Seeing Beyond the Obvious and the External

I love being a father, and I love my daughters Indigo and Azure dearly, but reading that study made me think about how different their experiences will be from mine, based on their gender. If girls are judging themselves primarily on their physical traits, then they must be doing the same thing to one another. I hope that by spending time with my girls and sharing my love of art with them, I might help offset any loss of self-esteem they may experience because of those who base their values on the superficial and not the consequential. The study also made me think about boys and men. We're constantly told that the roving eyes that once made us good hunters now get us into trouble with women. We too base so many of our judgments about women on their appearance. As men, we have to be careful not to form too much of our opinion of a woman on her looks. In some ways, it can seem as if we are going against our nature by doing that, but we need to.

Letting women know that you value them enough to treat them in the same way you would want to be treated, and that you don't simply view them as sexual objects, is the right thing to do. It may pay off for you in other, important ways down the line. I know that if I had to make a decision about who to hire and who to reject as an applicant, the person who acted appropriately in an office or interview setting would get the nod over someone who had the roving eye. What if we all thought about ourselves differently—broke the old-fashioned barriers that cause us to undervalue ourselves and one another—and put value on qualities like intelligence, integrity, charity, or even our sense of humor? Throw a healthy dose of respect for yourself and others in the mix and you are on your way.

Walking the Walk

One of the major ways that we can increase our value is by refining our skills and abilities and then demonstrating those talents to others. When I was a kid, my artwork was entered in schoolwide and citywide competitions, and those times I won or earned praise for my artwork, I felt so much better about myself. When I was twelve, one of my pieces—a drawing of a rural snowy landscape—was chosen to represent our school in front of all of Cleveland. You have no idea how that made me feel about myself, how much it increased my value in my own eyes and those of my peers. More important, my art was the one thing that my foster parents appreciated about me. As harsh as they were, I was still like any kid some of the time. I wanted their approval, and my art was just about the only way that I could earn it. I can still, after all these years, picture Reverend and Mizz Pickett's faces creasing into smiles of approval when I showed them one of my better drawings. Though their words of praise were faint, they couldn't mask their admiration. Even better, their review only confirmed what I already knew. I didn't need them to tell me what I'd done was good; I had already formed that opinion of my work. I wanted their approval, but I didn't have to have it. What are your talents and abilities? Set aside what your peers might want you to do on any given afternoon, or what your parents have pushed you to do or become. What are the things that in your private time give you a sense of satisfaction and self-worth? What's your passion?

Try with a Little Help

The distinction between wanting and needing the approval of others is an important one. I do believe it's important to hear that inner voice telling you that you have worth, but that doesn't mean you have to always go it alone. I was an extremely shy kid, and the competitive world of the classroom and my relative silence made it easy for me to be overlooked and underappreciated—both of which definitely contributed to lowered self-esteem. We all like to be recognized, and whenever I was working on a drawing or painting and someone noticed my work and praised it, my self-esteem rose. That's a natural response, but as the years went by, I learned through experience that I could do the same thing for myself. I could be open to the praise that motivated me without relying on it to keep moving forward.

As kids, we spend almost as much time at school as we do at home, and so teachers, administrators, and other adults at school play a huge role in helping us see ourselves as valuable. I know that in my case, by the time I was Indigo's age, I was only just beginning to really be consciously aware that I had any value. One of the people who contributed so much to that awareness was my teacher Mrs. Profit (there's one of those money words again; but there's no dollar amount that can describe how much she did for me) who I had, at her request, as a teacher in fourth, fifth, and sixth grades. If you've read *Finding Fish*, then you already know how enormously influential Mrs. Profit was and how if it weren't for her, my life could have turned out very differently. One thing that Mrs. Profit did that helped me to value myself was to assign me a seat between two of the prettiest and most popular girls in the school, Janine King and Janice Womack.

Mrs. Profit understood that developing social skills was as important a part of our education as our classroom work. You already know that I was so shy that I tried to buy myself some attention. The prospect of being popular was beyond the realm of my imagination. Mrs. Profit knew that unless I came out of my social exile (both self- and externally imposed), life was going to remain difficult for me. That's where Janine and Janice unknowingly served as my tutors. All I had to do was sit there and listen to these two chatterboxes, and I was attending a master class in the art of conversation. (I can say that about the two of them since we are still in contact with one another. In fact, I just spoke to Janice last week.) I wasn't really capable of joining in on their chatfests, but I could at least listen in and observe how it was done. In my mind I'd interject a few witticisms and a bon mot or two (although at the time if you had asked me what a bon mot was, and spelled it for me, I would have told you that it was breed of dog) but the reality was that I managed to get out a few words now and again. Removed from the deprivation of the Pickett house, I had a teacher who was looking out for me and trying to help and understand me. And I also had two classmates who could act as examples of what it was like to socialize in a fun and nonthreatening way. For a lot of young men, finding a voice sharing your thoughts with others can feel like a challenge.

Along with knowing what you like and who you are, and being able to name your positive qualities, it's equally important to know what your weaknesses are. I was very aware that I was shy and uncommunicative, and Mrs. Profit's strategy to put me near two talkative and outgoing girls had the desired effect. We all know that having good role models is important to our development. Mrs. Profit was wise enough to understand that I didn't just need adult role models; I also needed peer models whom I could emulate if I chose to. Are there peers around you doing the kinds of things you'd like to, as well? Would joining the drama club or other after-school groups take you out of your comfort zone and expose you to some of the skills you need? What group activities or clubs are in your community that can introduce you to the right kinds of peers?

Mistakes I've Made

Even though I was painfully shy, I still craved interaction with the people around me. Fitting in with my peers became increasingly important to me as I grew older. Although I believed in my heart I was valuable, I wouldn't be happy unless I had that value validated by my peers, the kids around me at school and in the neighborhood. But instead of choosing the best role models, I concentrated on the kids who were the most popular. And in those days, the crowd I wanted to hang around with were frequently the ones who got into the most trouble.

One winter, when I was about ten, and looking back now, at the height of my neediness, I was hanging out with a crew of other boys—Jessie, Fat Kenny, and Michael were the group's most prominent members. We were just standing around on a street corner talking and laughing. I was feeling pretty good about myself at that point. I was involved in the give-and-take of boyish banter, trading insults and put downs, finally able to pay my dues in the currency of kids, free of my stuttering hesitancy. Despite the cold weather, the warmth of acceptance cloaked me—I couldn't have cared less about the threadbare plaid wool shirt jacket I was wearing. A wet Lake Erie snow had fallen, and the temperature had clawed its way past the freezing mark, turning the precipitation into swollen slush the color of milk chocolate.

I was feeling pretty good about hanging with my "friends," and also about the fact that I was wearing a pair of combat boots my foster mother had picked up at the secondhand shop she owned and operated. They had the high sheen of what I would later know as parade gloss, and they were about the nicest item of clothing I had. I was proud of those boots, and their steel toes made me impervious to my friend's attempts to stomp my feet into numb submission. In some respects, I wish that they had. As was typical, I wasn't at the center of attention. Something told me that I wanted to be, and as cars passed, an idea came to me.

"Watch this," I said. I'd spotted a Buick Electra 225, what guys in the neighborhood would later refer to as "a deuce and a quarter," coming toward our gathering. The car slowed for a traffic light that had just turned red, its impressive front grille riding high. It stopped just beyond me, and I took a few quick running steps and kicked the car's right rear quarter-panel with the toe of my sturdy boot. The echoing report of leather-wrapped steel was loud enough to be heard above the city's din. The startled driver responded instantly, but I was already running, followed by my buddies. We ran a block and then stopped to look back. The man hadn't bothered to pursue us. He was inspecting his car. I knew that I'd put a large dent in it, and even from that distance I could see his distress. He stood for a moment with his hands clasped on top of his head. He leaned back and seemed to beseech the heavens to deliver him from that evil.

My buddies were all laughing. Fat Kenny clapped his hand on my shoulder and issued the highest of compliments, "Man, you crazy."

As soon as my foot made contact with the car, I was already beset by guilt. I had no idea of its value, how hard the owner had to work to earn the kind of money necessary to purchase it, but I did know this: I knew the Electra 225 was expensive and repairing the damage would cost a considerable amount. Still, I did briefly enjoy the attention I received, and the thrill of having done something like that was electrifying. Unfortunately, neither the attention nor the thrill lasted. By the end of that afternoon, I'd watched them play the game of "can you top this" in an escalation of our sick efforts to impress one another. I'd wanted the guys to see me as their equal, if not their better, and I'd risen in their estimation temporarily. But I also realized that the stakes were continually raised. Was I capable of earning my stripes by doing even more outrageous things? Eventually, I opted out of the game. I had no taste for it, and though the Picketts never found out what I'd done, my wretched feelings were punishment enough.

Imitation, Confidence, and Productivity

I don't know how Mrs. Profit would have felt about my choice of peers, but I can guess. She wanted me to come out of my shell, but I'd gone too far. Her idea of influence was to tell me to go home and watch an old Cary Grant movie. As dapper and charming as Mr. Grant was, his style was out of my league and he was nearly an alien considering the realities of day-to-day life in Cleveland. The question I often asked myself was, *If you don't have those traits, then how do you get them?* Change is difficult for all of us, and in time I devised some strategies for making changes that would increase my value. In general, the catchphrase, "fake it until you make it," holds a lot of wisdom. Few of us are born with complete, arrogance-free confidence. When we're valuable, we have confidence. We have to earn our confidence through success, but unless you've already succeeded, how do you get confidence? Well, that's where the faking it comes in. "Faking it" has such negative connotations that most of us don't like the term. But the truth is, most of us have also likely faked it before we succeeded at some endeavor. Maybe "imitate" is a better choice of words, but even that brings up images of comedians doing impersonations and acting the clown. No, I wasn't going to go around my neighborhood talking like Cary Grant—and how could I even begin to dress like him?

The practice of imitating or copying is a tried-and-true method of instructing artists. Even the most talented art student spends hours in museums copying the works of the great masters. The hope is that by copying what the best have done, an artist, in this case a painter, will one day create a work of art as inspired and original and brilliant as those that hang in the Louvre in Paris or in Los Angeles at the Getty Museum. I have always loved museums, and they inspire me. I like to walk among the best that civilization has produced over the ages. And it doesn't just have to be paintings or sculpture. Many museums include design collections that might feature cars or furniture or films. So whether its paying attention to something small, like how two girls in my class interacted socially, or walking humbly among the finest artifacts and artwork at the museum nearest you, we can all learn how to increase our value by surrounding ourselves with those things toward which we aspire. While we might not always be able to mechanically copy an example the way a painter does, and we shouldn't reduce imitation to the form of mimicking another, learning by example is essential.

Momentum

I've touched on a lot of activity that involves thinking: Think about who you are and who you want to be. Think about the people around you and the kind of influence they have on your life. But thinking can only take you so far, right? You're not going to just think yourself into the president's chair at a corporation or a doctor's set of scrubs. Being productive also increases our value—both our sense of self-worth and in the eyes of others. I know that sometimes, as a writer, the words don't come easily to me on a particular day. The screen may remain blank, and even though I'm thinking hard about a scene that I have to rewrite, I don't have much to show for it. It would be easy to think that I wasn't doing anything of real value then. I know that isn't true, but I sometimes can't help but feel that way. How do I combat that feeling of decreased value on days when I'm not producing the kind of results that I feel I should be?

The answer is simple: I do something. I make progress on some other project around the house or in my writer's room. I'm still very much a kid at heart in a lot of ways, and I like to surround myself with fun things. One of them is scale-model cars. If my writing isn't going particularly well, I may step away from the computer and get to work assembling a car. I like the idea that when I'm through working on the model car, I can see tangible progress from my efforts. I'm closer to completion than when I started. That feels important to me, and the sense of accomplishment increases my value.

I also love to listen to and play music. I have a bass guitar (I didn't make that part up; I have a Fender Marcus Miller Jazz bass guitar) and if I'm not making progress on a script, I'll pick up the guitar and play for a bit. Learning a new piece, but especially playing along with a song on my iPod and figuring out the chords, gives me the same kind of satisfaction as scale modeling. I hear myself getting better or making it farther through a song than before and that makes me feel like my time has been well spent. Music brings beauty into the world, and making music instead of just passively listening to it (though there's nothing wrong with simply appreciating music) enhances that beauty. I also paint. So it's not all about work, and it's important as you develop to be well-rounded. Sometimes we reach a point in our daily activities or our studies or our careers where we hit a roadblock. Having other outlets for your personal expression is a good way to maintain your value. We've touched on thinking, and on doing, and then there's doing for others, which is an essential part of character.

Being of Service

I have a very clear recollection of when I made the connection between being of service to others and feeling valuable. Again, I was ten years old, and it was one of those thickly humid summer days in Cleveland that had me feeling like someone had taken LePage's Paste and used it to coat my skin. I was walking down 105th Street, just a block or so from the Picketts' house in Glenville. School wasn't in session, and I'd done all the day's chores Mizz Pickett had assigned me. I was granted a leave of absence from the house. I think it was so warm that Mizz Pickett was glad to have one less body warming up the house. I was walking along, dragging a stick over the sidewalk, enjoying the sound of it scraping and then bouncing over the cracks. Something caught my eye and I looked across the street to a front yard where I saw an arcing spray of water rainbowing across the lawn. My first thought: sprinkler! My second thought: sticking my head in that cooling spray. When I crossed the street, my hopes were dashed. Instead of a sprinkler, I saw a woman I didn't know holding her thumb over a garden hose. She was sending a spray of water over window blinds she'd draped over a chair.

To me, she seemed old, and the arcing spray I'd seen must have happened when she took her hand, still holding the hose, and lifted it to wipe her brow. I briefly considered turning back around, but I paused midstreet before jogging the rest of the way toward her.

"Can I help you with that?" The words came out of my mouth almost on their own.

When she didn't respond at first, I thought that those weightless words had been carried away by the wind.

I repeated my question.

The woman turned toward me and put one hand to her chest, "Oh, you scared me."

I moved my eyes from hers to a metal bucket that was frothing over with soapy water. The handle of a brush, much like the one we used to scrub the toilets at Mizz Pickett's, bobbed in the turbulent water like a buoy.

"I could help." I pointed toward the brush, and she nodded.

I spent the next half hour scrubbing those wooden blinds, the piney smell of Murphy's Oil Soap working its way up my nostrils. It was not unpleasant, neither the work nor the scent, and the two of us didn't exchange many words, just a "thank you so much" and a "you're welcome" before I headed for home.

Of course, when I got there, Mizz Pickett gave me hell for my wet shoes and the footprint I left on the welcome mat. Even her rude greeting could not bring me down from the high I felt. As much as I fussed about being forced to do all kinds of work around the Pickett household, I felt a wonderful lightness for having volunteered to help a stranger. I enjoyed that sensation so much, I woke up the next day craving more of it. I walked back to her house, and tentatively knocked on the screen door. Through a gray haze of mesh, I saw the blinds lying across the dining room table, dangling down to the floor.

I spent the next half hour hanging those blinds, standing atop that same table in my bare feet. Mizz Pickett would have skinned me alive for such an act of impertinence. But instead, this woman stuffed three dollars in my hand when I was done helping her and on my way to the front door. I thanked her, and when I stepped out into the bright sunlight, the day's glare stabbed at my eyes. That wasn't the only pain I was feeling. Something didn't feel right about taking that money. After all, she hadn't asked for my help. That feeling of lightness that I'd experienced the day before when I'd freely offered my help and it had been freely accepted was replaced by the sensation of appearing to have been opportunistic. I'd honestly just wanted to help her because she seemed like she needed it. I could not imagine a woman of her age clambering up onto a table and leaning out into space to fit those blinds back in their holders.

Years later when I was in the navy, the desire to be of service took other forms. At every opportunity, I would volunteer to go to orphanages, hospitals, any place where my presence might lighten someone's burden, even if only temporarily. When you don't give of yourself to others, it's an indication you feel that you don't have anything to offer. In other words, you view yourself as worthless, and that's a terrible mind-set to have. Real value can be, but rarely is, about money changing hands between people. The value that passes from one person to another and back is the effort we put into taking care of and helping one another out, especially in times of need.

Chart Your Progress

Determining and increasing your value as a human being is a growth process. As kids, we like to stand up against a wall or a doorjamb and measure our increasing height (no standing on tiptoes!). Or we stand back-to-back with friends or classmates to see who is taller. I can remember as a kid trying to touch the bottom of the basketball net as a way of measuring myself against other boys. Later on, anyone who could touch the rim or even dunk a basketball held a special place of honor. Testing ourselves physically like that became a part of our daily routine. As I said before, boys are doers, and that's how we measure ourselves. But that's not the only way we should assess ourselves and our progress.

I think we should do the same thing with our sense of worth. Talk about it, talk about your interests, your talents, your desires. As those dreams and those skills expand, put a mark higher up on the wall, see that your vision of yourself is greater than the dimensions of your physical body.

When I was in school, a science teacher told us that experts had determined the dollar value of all the chemicals that make up the human body. I can't remember the amount he said we were worth back then. I tried to find the answer, but the nearest I came to my school days was a 1985 estimate of $1.98. I also calculated that in 2008 that amount would be $4.50. Obviously, the value of a human life is far greater than a few dollars, and we need to understand that. In a way, this is not much different than those couple of dollars I was worth to my foster parents. Were they simply being paid to store the chemicals that were Antwone Fisher? I keep coming back to the idea that it is what is inside us that is important, but that only tells part of the story. I know that you can't put a dollar amount on our value, but I hope you understand that you are worth something, often far more than what other people are willing to appraise you at, but there are also things that you can do to change their estimation of your worth.

But before you can do any of that, you've got to take stock of yourself. By inventorying those things that you can do for yourself and for others, by finding others whose qualities and characteristics you admire and aspire to discover and enhance in yourself, your value will rise in your own eyes. There is no timetable to which you must keep, but since there are no deadlines other than those you impose on yourself, why not get started now?

CHAPTER TWO

PAY ATTENTION TO YOUR INTUITION

I don't know if it was because no one else seemed to be very concerned about my survival in this world, but I grew up with a keen sense of my own mortality and all the possible ways in which I could be hurt. Maybe it was the steady diet of war-centered shows and Westerns I watched on the television. In their own dramatic fashion, they taught me that life was often hard and cruel and it was easy to be gunned down. I hope that your life is free from these kinds of worries—it's a pretty heavy load to carry as a little kid. As you know, there were some bad people in my life and my fears could get the better of me. These were dark forces, and I could never be certain whether one of them might sweep me away. I certainly didn't think that there was an adult or authority figure who could come to my protection. In the face of a very real struggle I endured as a child, I realized that protecting myself was extremely important.

As a result, I developed a pretty keen survivor's instinct. Even as a young boy, my sense that some things were safe and others unsafe was usually right. A lot of people have written or spoken to me about an incident in my memoir, when Mizz Pickett's grandchildren and two of her other foster children were playing with matches and set the house on fire. I was supposed to be napping, and worried that I would get in trouble for not doing as I was told. I stayed upstairs even after I smelled and saw smoke. My instinct told me to get out of there, but all I could think of was the whipping I would get if I didn't follow orders. That's how bad things were at one point in my childhood. Sensing that the house was on fire and that my chance of being caught up in that fire was becoming more and more real by the second, I could not bring myself to flee the house because disobeying Mizz Pickett would lead to immediate and brutal punishment. I guess that an adult really can beat the good sense out of a child, but after that incident and my narrow escape, I listened to the voice that told me to do whatever I could to protect myself and forget all the rest.

When I first met another boy from the neighborhood named Jessie, my antennae picked up warning signals immediately. They told me that this was a kid I should be afraid of. Jessie was one of those neighborhood guys (he was only ten when I met him but he seemed older) with a crazed look in his eye. If I was willing, at least once, to kick a car to gain some street nobility, then Jessie was the kind of kid who'd go to a local car dealership and kick an entire row of cars. Still, as much as my intuition told me to avoid Jessie and to fear him, like everyone else I knew, I was drawn to him. His bravado was a form of charisma under whose spell we all fell.

I had to literally fall under Jessie to realize just how powerful he was. We all liked to wrestle, and I thought I had some pretty good moves. I always held my own against the other guys and that earned me a bit of much needed respect. One day I was with a couple of neighborhood boys when Jessie came around the corner. Fat Kenny spotted him, and he urged the two of us to wrestle. I was feeling pretty good about myself, so I shrugged my shoulders and looked at Jessie and said, "Let's go." We stood a few feet apart, and Jessie's wicked grin sliced his face. In unison, we said, "One. Two. Three." Before I knew it, I was on the ground with Jessie on top. Most kids started out by trying to grab your arms, but Jessie had shot himself at my legs and taken me down without a struggle. As I lay there with my arms wrapped around my head to ward off the blows that Jessie was raining down on top of me like a fierce summer storm, I realized that I needed to be friends with Jessie. I couldn't afford to avoid him or try to outdo him; I had to utilize his forces in my interest.

Jessie truly was a force of nature and was as unpredictable, too. That was what really set him apart. He wasn't a bully in the traditional sense—someone who you know is always going to be after you. Today, I understand that Jessie was mercurial—as slippery as that chemical substance, mercury, from which the adjective gets its name. If I was able to contain him, just as mercury in a thermometer proves useful, then I could benefit from his presence. Along with his unpredictable nature, Jessie was dangerous because he was completely without fear. My intuition told me that Jessie would not live long, and I was eventually proved correct. I knew that as fearless and unpredictable as Jessie was, there were others out there who were equally dangerous and who possessed those same traits in an even greater quantity than Jessie. Hopefully you don't have someone nearby who was as dangerous as Jessie, but we all know people who are capable of "stirring things up." Your intuition is going to tell you whether being near them is wise, or even if co-opting them in some way is better than having them as a potential enemy. Navigating these relationships and having an internal guide that helps you develop—or avoid—relationships is critical. Even life saving.

I'm glad that I listened to my intuition the day that Jessie was killed. This occurred after I had been to reform school and while I was homeless. I was playing basketball and Jessie told me to come with him. I had been crashing at his place, and I felt an obligation to him, but something in the back of my mind told me that I was better off finishing the game. I still wanted Jessie on my side, but I knew that in a very real way, he'd outgrown me. I can still picture Jessie standing in front of the mom-and-pop record store, his Stacy

Adams shoes polished to a high sheen, his maxi overcoat and his fedora making him look much older than he was. He did not have much regard for the law. His job in the maintenance department at the Cleveland Clinic helped him support himself. I was glad that I listened to my instincts and wasn't standing next to him when he was shot and killed, but I was sad that my instincts about Jessie's fate had proven to be correct. When I was homeless, when I was hanging out with Jessie, at that time I was at the bottom. This might seem a long way off from where you are now, and I hope it is. But I share my experiences from my time there so that you don't ever have to know what it feels like yourself.

Be a Punk, But Don't Show It

In my neighborhood, someone who was afraid was considered a punk. That was about the worst thing you could be, and though I felt fear and paid attention to it, I put up a façade of false bravado that kept me safe from scorn as well as violence. Feeling the fear was a good thing and alerted me to all kinds of potential dangers. Not showing my fear helped me to maintain control of myself and whatever situation I might be in—at least most of the time.

So when kids were doing things that I deemed potentially harmful, I made careful choices about whether or not to join them. Maybe I am a slow learner, but even those near-misses with the fire, with car kicking, and Jessie's wrestling didn't keep me from sometimes ignoring what my intuition told me was the best course of action.

My nearly overwhelming desire to connect with other people led me to do some stupid things. I've already told you that I stole pocket change and gave it to other kids at school so that they would like me. Because I lacked normal friendships and emotionally healthy relationships with my foster family and the other kids at home, I seized nearly every opportunity I could to get someone on my side. When I was nine or ten years old, a new family moved into the house next door to ours. One of their children was a boy about my age named James. I figured that he was a new kid in the area and a prime candidate for me to befriend. I had proximity as an advantage, and so I showed him around the school, introduced him to the other kids, and generally bent over backward to be a good buddy.

Another Mistake

Something about James seemed a little off to me. As nice as I was to him, he always seemed to have this sly grin, and I had the impression that a lot of the time he was rolling his eyes whenever I said something. It was just a momentary flicker that hinted somehow he was just tolerating me, using me to ease his transition from new kid on the block to establishing himself as a somebody. I too easily dismissed that feeling in the pit of my stomach telling me something wasn't quite right. It was good to have someone to hang out with, and I told myself I was probably just being overly suspicious.

One day James and I wandered the streets together. Never a good beginning to a story, right? Our momentum carried us out of our neighborhood and into an unfamiliar section of the city. I noted that only briefly; because I was so caught up in having someone to talk to and to spend the day with that it didn't matter where we were or what we were doing. At one point, we were stopped at a corner waiting for the light to change so that we could cross. A steady stream of traffic passed by, the rushing sound of tires interrupted by a regular thump as cars passed over a patch in the road where a work crew had spread a patch of shiny asphalt.

Once the light changed, we marched across the wide avenue.

James pointed and said, "Look." In front of a storefront sat a row of bicycles. I looked up and saw a sign, a pair of scissors and a comb and the silhouette of a woman, like the woman on the package of Camay soap but with a stacked beehive of hair all in neon. Beneath those images were the words, MISS DINAH'S CUT AND CURL. I was fascinated by the sign, but my friend's gentle nudge to my ribs with his elbow ended my contemplation.

"Let's take some bikes."

We'd just stepped onto the curb and were about fifteen feet from the parked bikes. I immediately thought, *No. No. I can't do that.*

He sensed my hesitation. "C'mon, man. We can ride them home. I don't feel like doing no more walking."

He took a couple of steps forward, but I was lagging behind purposefully. He turned to face me and his shoulders slumped, and he said, "Dag, Antwone. Ain't no big thing. You grab one and I'll grab one. Let's go!"

I tried to think of a reason why we shouldn't, but my mind was a jumble of images I tried to sort through. Why was there a comb on that sign and not a hair pick? The beehive reminded me of The Supremes and Diana Ross.

"C'mon," he said and started jogging toward the bikes.

My feet seemed to have a mind of their own. I trailed just behind him, and eventually caught and passed him. "Let's go. Let's go," he urged me on.

I grabbed the handlebars of the bike nearest to me and yanked it out of the line. Several of the other bikes clattered to the sidewalk. I jumped on the pedals and started pumping. I heard someone shouting at me to stop, but I put my head down and zoomed up the sidewalk, oblivious to the pedestrians. They scattered and I took the first turn I could off the main drag and down a side street. Just before I turned, I took a look back, and a group of boys was on the other bikes pursuing me. Even though what I was doing was totally wrong-headed and even criminal, my intuition and fear kicked into gear with nothing but self-preservation as a goal. I was so frightened by the idea of them catching me, that I don't think I ever pedaled a bike as fast as I did during that escape. Also, even though I'd been in a part of town I wasn't that familiar with, I managed to navigate in such a way that I wound up near my school. I was so focused on just getting away that I didn't have much time to think about what James had done to me: he'd set me up for the fall and hadn't even taken a bike himself. I fell for his prank all because I didn't listen to the voice in my head telling me that he wasn't somebody that I could trust. How stupid was I to have stolen that bike? I put myself and others in harm's way because I didn't have the self-confidence to turn James down.

I came flying onto the school parking lot, skidding and fishtailing to a stop. Quite a few kids from the neighborhood were gathered there playing basketball and crawling all over the playground equipment. I started to call their names, "Hey Michael! Hey Chris!" I looked out toward the street and saw that the pack that was chasing me had stopped and those kids were looking my way. I continued to call more names, and what my gut told me to do seemed to have the desired effect. Those other boys were afraid that I was going to round up my own posse and beat them down and take the rest of their bikes. My thoughts flickered back to the Westerns I watched where a posse might run into an outlaw's camp and a gunfight ensues. My pursuers slunked off, departing without a word. I'd expected at least an insult or two to be lobbed my way like a Molotov cocktail. I was thrilled that they were gone. A situation like that can easily spin out of control.

When the rush wore off, the sad reality set in. I had this bike that I didn't even want. I felt horrible about having stolen it. Just as bad, I felt miserable that I'd been tricked. I was kicking myself for thinking that James and I were going to be friends. I didn't really know him all that well, but I was so eager to have someone on my side that I was willing to overlook any suspicions that I might have had about him. I'd let him talk me into stealing a bike! I knew better than that.

So there I was on the playground parking lot with all these kids around wondering what I should do. I knew I couldn't take the bike home. At that point, James came running up to me. His face split by a huge grin, he said, "Alright, man. You got it! Cool! You got it! We can share riding it. You can use it one day, and I can use it the next."

I looked at him, completely startled. How unfair was that? Was that his plan all along, have me do the dirty work for him so that he could ride a bike.

"Man," I said, "why didn't you take a bike?"

"I was trying to distract them. Make your getaway easier."

Something told me that this was a lie, but still there was some logic to that explanation. I quickly realized that I had another issue to deal with. "You can have the bike. I don't want it."

"I can't have a bike. My parents aren't going to let me keep the thing."

I knew I had to get out of there. I started walking the bike toward my house, guilt and anger ratcheting in intensity with each sidewalk crack I passed over. I was hoping that no one would see me. One of the kids from the neighborhood, a short torsoed kid with long, lanky limbs and a big head, trotted up alongside me.

He asked me where I got the bike. I told him the truth. I'd stolen it. He said that he'd take it, and I let him have it. I walked the rest of the way home, my head on a swivel. I jumped every time I heard the sound of an approaching car. I did not rest well that night.

The very next day, I got caught. The boy who owned the bike and his father were driving around the neighborhood and they spotted me. I confessed everything to my foster parents. I told them that the big-headed kid up the street had the bike. When they went to get the bike from him it was too late. The big-headed kid had already stripped it down to just the bare frame. I stood there with my foster father and the boy and his father staring at that miserable sight.

The father turned to his son and said, "See what happens when you don't take care of your things? Why didn't you lock the bike up like I told you to?" He picked up what was left of the bike and said, "Here it is. This is yours."

They walked away and got into their car. I watched as the boy slumped in his seat as his father drove off. I felt so bad for him, but what could I say or do? I was the cause of his pain. What hurt me at that moment was that I would have rather have been friends with him instead of James. I'd certainly never have that chance now.

Refining My Skills and Understanding

As an adult, I look back at that mistake and note a lot of things. What strikes me is that the boy who took the bike off my hands was sophisticated enough in the ways of crime to know that he couldn't keep the bike whole. Like someone operating an automobile chop shop, he had that bike stripped of anything valuable overnight. There sure were some streetwise kids hanging out there back in the day.

Unfortunately, in life, there are just some lessons we have to learn the hard way. Whether it is our own mistakes, as it was in this instance, or circumstance dealing us a bad hand. Over time and with experience, I developed a kind of sixth sense about things. I became sensitive to the energy that people and places projected. There were often a lot of fights and goings-on after school, and toward the end of each day, I was like a doctor making his rounds. I would check the pulse of the place, trying to determine what was up. Were people in a good mood, had all the disputes been settled? Was there some lingering resentment that hadn't been resolved? Had the brief incident in the cafeteria at lunch time been settled to everybody's satisfaction? Had the jokes about somebody's mother crossed a line? In some ways, I was also like a dog. At the end of the day, I'd go from the school's vestibule where the radiators exhaled stale, humid breaths out into the fresh air. I'd raise my nose to the wind, sniffing to sense what was up. If I felt trouble was brewing, I'd take the long way home, along 105th Street. That way, I'd avoid most of the kids who walked along Parkwood Avenue. Most of the time when I took 105, my suspicions were confirmed the next day when I learned that Charles and his buddies and Robert and his fellas had gotten into it. I was glad to have avoided the possibility of being dragged into the melee.

I owed much of that intuitive sense to my foster family. I was constantly being warned not to go into anyone else's house. It wasn't that they altogether mistrusted other families, but as they told me, "You never know who's going to be over there." I was naïve and trusting in most ways, and the lure of someone's house nearly always overpowered my sense of caution. For example, my friend Robert had a slot car racing set at his house, and I had to see that thing and get a chance to play with it. Fortunately nothing bad happened to me on those forbidden visits. I guess that my foster parents knew what they were talking about; after all, it was within the four walls of their home that I was being abused. They knew that dark deeds could take place anywhere.

A Good Choice

Strange as it may seem, I'm glad that I grew up in an inner-city environment. It helped to sharpen my intuition. That point was driven home to me several years ago. The movie *Antwone Fisher* was finally close to being ready to go into production. Along with Denzel Washington, who was going to make his directorial debut working on the film, I was back in Cleveland with Todd Black, the producer and the man who really gave me the opportunity to be in this business. We were scouting locations back in my old neighborhood, the three of us just walking down the street, talking about the film and other things on our minds.

All of a sudden, Denzel stopped and put his arm out. He cocked his head to the side and his brow furrowed in concentration. I immediately froze and scanned the street for signs of danger. After a few more steps, Todd turned to us and saw us lingering behind. "C'mon guys," he waved us on. That's when I saw what Denzel was looking at. Five unsavory men were standing in a parking lot near a car, doing what appeared to be a drug transaction. When the men saw us they scrambled into the car and took off with tires squealing. They probably thought that we were undercover police officers. What else would they think when they saw a white guy standing with two black guys looking at them there in a black ghetto?

Todd looked at Denzel and me and said, "Wow! That was intense."

Denzel nodded and said, "You can never lose that edge, that street intuition."

Denzel had developed some of the same intuition as I had. I'm sure that Todd had never experienced inner city life and the kind of danger you anticipate around every corner.

A Good Choice Turns Even Better

The interesting thing about Todd is that he has a very good sense of people and their abilities even if he doesn't share my intuition of the streets. Also, I wouldn't have chosen to work with him if it weren't for my sense that he was someone who I could trust with my story. My intuition served me well. Hollywood and the film industry can be a very scary places, particularly for first-time writers. I'd decided to tell my story, and I'd written draft after draft of a screenplay. As an adult, after many years to digest and heal from the experiences I had as a boy, I heard a voice within me that finally wanted to speak. This was quite a step for a guy who could barely socialize with others early in life, but I was just at the beginning of this great adventure. Ironically enough, it was when I was in Los Angeles working as a security guard on the Sony Pictures studio lot that I decided that I wanted something more than being on the outside of the film industry. I also believed that my story was worth telling. I began taking screenwriting classes with a great guy named Chris Smith. Right away, I told him my personal story, and he suggested that I get in contact with his college roommate.

"He's a producer and he has a deal with Twentieth Century Fox." At first I was a little leery. I'd been around in Los Angeles long enough to know that while a lot of people were actually in the business, it wasn't possible that everyone was. It sometimes seemed as if almost everyone was a "producer." They can't all whip out a business card to prove it, but Chris shared with me his friend's contact information and, sure enough, he really was a producer. I figured that if he had the credentials then he was someone definitely worth meeting. I gave him a call and through his assistant, we set something up for a few weeks later. At that stage in my career my Hollywood intuition only extended as far as knowing who should be allowed on the premises of the movie lot where I worked and who shouldn't. I knew that people were always trying to sneak in to push a screenplay or to catch a glimpse of some star or another. In a way, I felt like I was sneaking into his office in Brentwood for that meeting. It was weird to be on the other side of things—instead of being the one inside the lot keeping folks out, I was outside trying to get in.

That feeling added to some of my apprehension, but when it came time to meet Todd, all those worries about the externals of being a relative newcomer centered on one thing: would anybody "get" my story. I wasn't wise enough in the ways of the film industry to have crafted what I later learned was called a pitch. I'd heard the term, but I wasn't able to really think through the clichéd idea that my story was *Rocky* meets *Roots* or whatever combination of successful movies I could come up with to encapsulate my life story. I went in there and just was myself—initially a very nervous self, but still just Antwone.

Mr. Black had a very nice office, nothing too fancy, but still as nice as anything I'd ever been allowed to take a seat in. We shook hands and he gestured toward a luxurious leather sofa. I sank down into it, and he joined me across from a low table. I liked that he didn't just take a seat behind his desk like a schoolteacher about to lecture a pupil. He sat across from me, and I appreciated that. We chatted for a bit, and then we got down to business.

"So, tell me, Antwone, what's your story?"

He leaned back in his seat like he was settling in.

"Well . . ." I launched in. At first I was just giving him the facts, a kind of dry recitation like I was reading off a grocery list. Then I tuned into my heart and also into him. I could see his facial expression change when I told him some of the details of my upbringing. His eyebrows rose and his pupils dilated with surprise. At other points, he'd nod or shake his head with empathy. That greatly encouraged me, but deeper than just those surface responses that I registered with my head, I could feel in my heart that this was somebody who did "get it." After awhile, I had the feeling that we were no longer in a brightly lit office, but that the two of us had been transported into a darkened movie theater and he was watching the incidents that made up my life unfold on the screen.

I also let my defenses down. Most of the time, I'd been a lot like the security guard at the gate of the studio. I didn't ever let anyone really inside my story, but with Todd I felt comfortable doing that. I raised the gate and let him inside and allowed myself to reexperience some of the emotions I had during both the tough and the good times. By doing that, I was able to tell my story in a way that really touched him. He ultimately did become the producer, and it was through his efforts that the movie was made. He really believed in me and in the project. He championed my cause and fought for me to be the screenwriter on the project, and helped cast the movie when the time came. The fact that Todd helped translate my script from words on the page to images on the screen and then emotions in other people's hearts still feels kind of like a miracle to me.

This could all happen because of some good luck and because I trusted my gut. When I met Todd in 1993, he had more than a few production credits to his name, some TV movies and films, but the connection we made at that first meeting convinced me that he was the one who would see my project through. Ultimately, I was proved right and the rest, as they say, is history.

But the rest of the story about how I learned to trust my own instincts and intuition isn't fully told yet. Learning to trust other people requires that you first learn to trust yourself. Just as I had to learn to think of myself as valuable, learning to trust myself, and consequently others, was an ongoing process.

Trusting Those Who Trust You

Enlisting in the navy did a lot to help me get to the point where I thought I was valuable enough to have a story that other people would not just want to hear but actually pay money to see. When I started my service, I was stationed aboard the USS *Schenectady* LST-1185. As an amphibious landing ship, it was used to transport marines and their equipment to wherever they were needed around the world. In order to get their tanks, jeeps, and personnel carriers on and off the ship, we had cranes and winches that lifted the heavy equipment. One rotating duty was called damage control. Because the ship and much of the equipment aboard was made of steel and was constantly exposed to the salty sea air, we had to be ever-vigilant in waging a war on corrosion. That meant doing all kinds of mainte-nance—or damage control.

The damage control petty officer came to me one day with an assignment. I was going to be responsible for maintaining one of the winches that would hoist millions of dollars of equipment onto and off of the ship. He explained that it was my responsibility to follow the instructions listed on a card. This card was specifically produced for that winch and spelled out its maintenance procedures. Because this maintenance was essential to the life of the ship, and if poorly performed, could lead to injury or the destruction of equipment, anyone responsible for that duty was under the threat of captain's mast (a courtlike setting for the purpose of delivering punishment), and dereliction of duty in the United States Navy was a serious offense. I had to be sure to lubricate various grease fittings compe-tently or face the consequences. When the petty officer was done with his explanation he asked me, "Do you understand?"

"I understand," I replied unconvincingly. He looked at me and frowned. I think he could tell that I was nervous. No one had ever entrusted me with a job that important before. I was thinking, *You can't rely on me to do a job this crucial.* I was well aware of the consequences of failure. If I didn't follow the maintenance card to the letter, the winch could seize up and the cable holding a tank in place could snap. It could either fall into the sea or crash onto the deck—killing my shipmates or certainly doing serious damage to the ship.

The petty officer looked at me and said, "You can and you will complete the task. Follow the instructions as spelled out on the maintenance card and the job will be done properly."

He was right about that. As it turned out, his faith in me helped me to have faith in myself. I did such a good job for the DCPO that I earned a very nice "atta-boy" from the chief petty officer of the division. I couldn't believe it. I was entrusted with an important task, and I had come through. Watching as we on-loaded and off-loaded that valuable equipment gave me a sense of pride I'd seldom felt before. It also started to confirm what I'd felt but had only occasionally had proof of: that I was a worthwhile and capable person. Later, when I was given the rate of ship's serviceman, I had an even greater sense that I could handle responsibility.

The petty officer was right about my apprehension and he was right to spell things out for me—particularly what the consequences of failure were. That put a different kind of fear in me, a fear that was more easily relatable than my uncontrollable fear of doing damage to millions of dollars in equipment. I could understand this kind of fear—the fear of getting in trouble for failing to do something well—in a way that I couldn't my fear of seeing tanks crashing into the sea. There's a subtle point of distinction between the two, but there's also the point of feeling the fear and doing the task anyway. Once I could put my fear into a more manageable context, I could perform my duty. My intuition told me that the job was an important one and that I'd better not mess up. That sense was doing battle with my weaker sense that I was someone who could be trusted. When I sat and thought about it, I realized that the navy had invested a lot of money in me and my training. Every day I was at work on a multimillion-dollar vessel. Everything I did on board that ship demonstrated the faith that the navy had placed in me. I just needed to have more faith in myself. I needed to do some of my own damage control and realize that all the things that I did every day, every bit of the training that I'd received, was maintenance work that would prevent me from rusting in place or breaking.

Later, when I earned the rate of ship's serviceman, I had an even greater sense that I could handle responsibility. All my experience in the navy was pointing me away from a poor conception of myself and allowing me to believe that what my gut had told me was true: I could achieve good things. At last, I was in an environment that wanted to see me succeed and could speak to me with words that weren't degrading and insulting.

Serving as a ship's serviceman was another important step for me. My foster mother took any opportunity she could to tell me that thieving was in my blood. She had never met my father but would erroneously say that he had been some kind of thief simply to insult me. As much as I tried to dismiss that idea as nonsense, I still had to wonder if maybe there was some truth to it. I had, after all, stolen a bicycle and a few other minor things around the house. Was I really a criminal dressing myself in a naval uniform? Were the voices in my head telling me that I was capable and trustworthy the words of an irredeemable liar?

As a ship's serviceman, it was my daily responsibility to collect all the money that had circulated on the ship that day. I was doing this aboard the USS *Cleveland* (LPD-7), another amphibious troop landing ship on which 300 sailors were stationed, with up to 900 additional marines once we embarked. All the money from the various vending machines (there were about seven aboard), all the proceeds from the sales at the ship's store—where sailors could buy anything from snacks to sweaters and everything in between—had to be counted, sorted, and deposited with the ship's disbursing officer. I can clearly recall sitting alone in the office counting all the money. I was surrounded by stacks of bills, and coins rolled into neat coils of currency. I'd look at it all and think, *They trust me with thousands of dollars every day.* Not once was I even tempted to take a dime of it, and that made me feel so good about myself. If other people could trust me, then I could trust myself. If I could trust myself, then I could trust the judgments I'd make about other people and about my own actions.

At the time I didn't really know what a feedback loop was, but I did notice that the more other people trusted me and the more I trusted myself, the more responsibilities I was given and the greater the subsequent trust placed in me. All of that served to offset the negative perceptions I'd formed about myself as the result of being told lies for so long: that I was the son of a no-account mother and a thieving father. I was learning that the blood that flowed through my veins wasn't tainted and impure or destined to lead me down the path of destruction. Instead, I had the growing sense that the lifeline I'd been cast to save myself from drowning in the sea of negative expectations had been secured already to a seaworthy vessel.

Trusting your gut is important. It can save you from doing something foolish or dangerous, but even more important, it helps you to better understand your value as a person. We often have to make snap judgments about people and situations based on very little evidence. Capitalizing on your own experience and the wisdom gained from those events is an important part of maturing into a man. I'm fortunate that through good and bad, I've been able to trust myself and what a select few others have told me about myself. Eventually that little voice in the back of your mind can come out and stand front and center, providing you with the guidance you need. Being a young man in the world presents some real challenges and will throw people your way who would see you forfeit your integrity, as James did to me, or open up a world of dangers because of their uncontrolled appetites, as with Jessie. Sometimes you are in situations where it is only you looking out for yourself, and what you decide in an instant can affect you far beyond that moment. Listen to your gut, and if it is telling you that what you are doing is not right, then follow those instincts. Even if you make mistakes, as I did, you are still capable of making the right choices and hanging with the right crowd.

CHAPTER THREE

GETTING YOUR CLEAN ON

While your head is filled with questions about where your life is going, let's get you busy on making some changes to your life that are a little more concrete. These things will help you establish who you are in the world, but they are hopefully easier to identify and implement than the big-picture questions about who you want to be and where you want to go. At some point later in life, I became aware that in neglecting me, the Picketts had failed to do many things that would help me make the transition from being a boy to being a man. And some of the things they did teach me were for the wrong reasons. Or I was forced to do them out of fear and humiliation, not because I ever understood their underlying value. For example, I might have been told to bathe because I was filthy and I smelled like an animal, and I was then compelled to take a bath that contained Clorox bleach diluted in water. It's amazing I ever took a bath again once I escaped. But as you become a man, or as you desire to be the kind of man others look up to, the way you live your life is part of the program. I was thinking about some of these issues when I was out walking with my wife the other morning.

Every morning after my wife and I drop our girls off at school, we take a walk around the cul de sac at the end of our block. At that hour of the morning, the air still holds the ocean's overnight coolness. Many of our neighbors have their lawn sprinklers going, and it's as if the whole world is clean and fresh from its ritual of renewal. Our stroll gives us a chance to talk about our plans for the day, to share with each other quiet moments away from the kids, our thoughts and concerns, free from interruptions by the phone. By being outside of the house, we can shed whatever filled our heads in the house and think about the new day. When we return home and shut the door, it's like we're back in our sanctuary and whatever we don't want to follow us back into the house is left on the outside.

Since I've been an adult, I've acquired the habit of removing my shoes whenever I come into the house. I first picked up on the idea of removing my shoes indoors when I was stationed in Sasebo, Japan. I love Japanese culture and the cleanliness and orderliness of its society. I believe that in terms of hygiene and a respect and care for the body, Japanese society can serve as a model for the rest of the world. Removing my shoes when I come home is also, in my mind, a show of respect. Living in urban Southern California like we do, I don't have to worry about tracking mud and snow in the house. Although we do have carpets and floor mats inside of every doorway that leads outside the house, I still think about the things that I could have stepped on or into while outside and cringe a little bit.

I'm no germphobe or whatever you call someone who must compulsively be clean; I simply remember what it was like living on Cleveland's mean streets. I know that people and animals dispose of a lot of things out on the streets and sidewalks, and I don't want to track any of that inside my house. I don't think that I'm fanatical, just practical. I'm also being respectful of the work my family does keeping our house clean. As I mentioned, the act of cleaning was drummed into me by the Picketts—like it or not; do it or get whipped. Every Saturday was housecleaning day, and I spent so many hours with a rag and a bottle of Lysol pine cleaner scrubbing away at the floors and baseboards of that house that I knew the location of every nail and knot in the wood. To be honest, I never minded those chores much. At least I knew what was expected of me and was largely left alone while I did it.

There was also an aspect of making sure everything was in proper order that appealed to me. As a kid, and particularly as a foster child who lived with a man and a woman who were happy one minute and furious the next only to change again minutes later, I was used to being in control of very few situations. When you are the victim of someone else's various whims and fancies, you're grateful for whatever bit of self-determination you can have, even if it means only the degree to which your environment is clean and well maintained.

Being inclined toward order to offset the chaos that was my world with the Picketts, I very much took to the military. Navy life was all about order and routine. I liked the predictability of the schedule. I needed to live in an environment in which expectations were clearly spelled out and consequences for failure to live up to those expectations and rewards for meeting them were consistently handed out. I've come to the conclusion that my believing and treating myself as someone of value was a natural extension of my desire to have control over my life. I'll write more about my life in the navy and the sense of order I learned there in a later chapter.

Working from the Outside In

So far, I've written a lot about reordering my life and how my self-perception evolved over the years. Those were all internal changes—changes that only I was aware of for the longest time, some changes that occurred without my even realizing. I think that fundamentally, you have to start there. Your personality, your sense of self and self-worth, are the foundations of who you are and who you will be. But my naval training brought a new and much needed perspective to my life: that who you are matters from the outside in, as well. And as I touched on earlier, while the Picketts were happy to compel me to polish their floors and clean their walls, they really could not have cared less whether or not I knew how to make myself a presentable individual. The fact of the matter is appearances do matter. In military lingo, if you are squared away (if you have a neat and clean appearance), that will translate into how you think about yourself and consequently how you behave. In many ways, the two are inseparable—the internal and the external. I remember how the comedian Billy Crystal used to do an imitation of the Latin actor Fernando Lamas. Crystal would have him say, "You look mahvelous." And then he'd go on to add, "It's better to look good then to feel good." I'd have to add that to feel good is to look good and vice versa.

I'm sure you've heard the expression "never judge a book by its cover." Well, in theory that may be true, but in practice, your appearance is all that anyone meeting you for the first time has to judge you on. To bring that analogy about books into the here and now, with my *Finding Fish* and now *A Boy Should Know How to Tie a Tie,* which you hold in your hands, my publishers put a lot of time and energy and talent into selecting the art and typography for the cover. Why did they do that? Because in this world in which thousands of books compete for your attention, a well-executed cover will get you to pick a book up and, hopefully, purchase it. In the world of business, when you are trying to sell yourself to an employer, for example, the same is true of how competitive, and in a sense superficial, things are. If your appearance initially draws the right kind of attention, makes the kind of statement about you that is appealing to prospective employers, then chances are, all other things being equal, you are considered a better candidate than someone who is less appealing. It's true that those are very subjective judgments that people will be making about your abilities, but the hard truth of the matter is that those kinds of assessments are rendered all the time. You can rant and rave about the injustice of that reality all you want—all the way to a lesser job for which you are overqualified.

Think about how you look—we'll also get to how you act—as your calling card or your business card. Just as a business card provides someone who receives it all the essential information about you—your title, the company you work for, your contact information—so does your overall appearance. Employers are looking for someone who is the "complete package," just as prospective friends and mates are, so you have to think about how you are going to present yourself in the most positive manner.

You may think that how you dress is a reflection of your mood on a particular day, and that can be true. Every time you make a choice about what clothes to wear, how you wear your hair, whether or not you go clean shaven or scruffy, you are making a statement to the world about yourself. When you are full of confidence about a killer presentation you've prepared for school or work, you might take a little extra time getting dressed. You think about yourself at the front of the room with all eyes on you and you bask in that daydream. Conversely, if you are weeks behind in your work and you'd just as soon disappear into the wallpaper at the office, you give little thought to the mismatched pants and shirt you pull from your closet. I like the expression "I just threw something on" because it speaks volumes about how people think about themselves and the impression they make. People use the expression to make it seem as if they put no thought into their appearance. What they don't realize is that consciously deciding not to put thought into their appearance is actually a way of putting thought into it. Life is all about choices, and when you decide to hide behind "I threw something on," what you're really saying is,

"I don't care." If you don't care, then that means you aren't valuing yourself, and if you're not valuing yourself, I can promise you no one else is going to value you. In my life, not even my mother or father would assign me the I-don't-care-I'm-not-worth-anything value. Don't take it for granted if your mother sees the world in you as you leave the house with your pants hanging down near your ankles or wearing your beat-up old baseball cap. Not everyone is going to see you through your mother's eyes.

Of course, I realize that sometimes we might say we threw something on as a way of deflecting attention from the care and precision with which we put ourselves together. I know that we sometimes use that line as a way to make it seem as if we aren't vain—it's a variation on the "This old thing? I've had it for years. Just came across it in the closet." I have some friends that if I were to believe everything they told me about their clothes, the last time they made a purchase was some time in the 1990s. I see people playing the "don't-notice-me-I-want-to-be-noticed!" game all the time. No one likes to be thought of as vain or arrogant, but I can't really think of any time when someone's clothing choice made that statement—generally it's how the person wears those clothes or how they present themselves and how they behave that makes us think that way about them.

You can look just as bad in a $5,000 Italian suit as you can in a $99 suit. You can look good in either of those, too. It's often said that clothes make the man, but I really think that the man makes the clothes. We've all seen someone look uncomfortable and unattractive in a tuxedo because of how out of sorts it makes him *feel*.

It's Not What You Have But How You Take Care of It

From my earliest days in school, I was very aware of my appearance. My foster parents didn't provide me with much, and as a keen observer, I noticed many of the things I mentioned earlier. I was acutely aware that the popular kids were frequently the best dressed. I don't know if it was their popularity that made what they wore so cool in my eyes or if it was the cool clothes that made them popular. Cause and effect didn't matter to me very much back then—I simply noted that the kids with the latest styles were the kids at the center of a group in the hallways or cafeteria. With my limited choices and means, I wasn't ever going to be able to have what they had. If you want to see the kinds of things guys were wearing when I was entering my teens, watch reruns of *Good Times*, *Welcome Back, Kotter*, or *What's Happening!* on cable TV. Maybe it's not such a terrible thing in retrospect that I didn't have them, but I craved those styles back then, when they were out of reach.

What I clearly remember were the 100 percent rayon shirts in bold prints that so many of my classmates wore. Paired with flared or bell-bottom jeans and a wide belt, that's what was happening in the halls of my school. Just like today, your jeans said a lot about who you were, and Levis were definitely cool, and Wranglers and—even worse—Sears Toughskin jeans were not. It's funny to think how Levis have already been in and out and back in fashion since before I was a kid. It just shows you how fleeting fashion can be. But that doesn't mean that dressing appropriately isn't the right thing to do.

Because I couldn't be too picky about what I wore, I had to be careful with how I wore my clothes. One of the great discoveries of my life, and one that I sometimes think was a lifesaver, was spray-on starch. No matter how threadbare, torn, or tattered my jeans became, a can of spray starch and a hot iron did a lot to give me the look I wanted. Designer jeans weren't really in fashion until later, so that wasn't the look I was after; instead, I simply wanted to project neat, clean, and well cared for. I can still smell the pungent odor of burning starch and the hiss and sizzle of the iron as the hot metal came in contact with the wet spray. Knowing that I was going to be wrinkle free with razor-sharp creases in my pants made me feel good about myself, and when you look good, you . . . well, you know the rest.

I don't want to spend too much time talking about fashion and clothes. (I'll spend much more time on the subject in a later chapter.) I just want to emphasize the point that no matter what your financial condition, you can look good. The key is to be presentable. It costs very little to do if you are willing to compromise sometimes, and you have the tools to get it done. Asking for a can of spray starch was a heck of a lot easier than asking for a new pair of jeans. Demonstrating to Mizz Pickett that I cared about and cared for the clothing I had, did make her look at me in a slightly different way. Maybe I wasn't as irresponsible as she thought. By presenting myself to her as someone who cared, she may have been willing to care about my needs a bit more—just a bit, but that was better than her caring not at all. In a way, paying attention to my clothes back then was a variation on the idea that sometimes it's appropriate to fake it until you can make it. I didn't have much in the way of new clothes, but I could make my old ones look as new as possible. One day I'd be able to afford those new things; until then, I had to make do.

Making Yourself Presentable: Your Hands

I mentioned Japan's culture was one I admired when I was stationed there. Given my desire to find order in my personal life through cleanliness, the emphasis that the Japanese put on good hygiene was one that immediately resonated within me. I probably assumed that my fellow sailors placed a similar emphasis on hygiene. The navy insisted that we care for our clothing and our personal appearance with an almost demonic attention to detail. (I found it close to heavenly: the one time a cliché—you know, the one about cleanliness being next to Godliness—seemed really appropriate to me.) But one night I was out with a group of sailors at a karaoke bar in the Agasaki Cho district of Sasebo City. One of my shipmates whom I didn't know well at all came out of the restroom. He was making his way toward our table when I heard someone say in heavily accented English, "Wash your damn hands."

I was shocked for a couple of reasons. The Japanese are generally very respectful, so to hear someone swear and embarrass someone like that was really out of place. I also didn't know that this woman—it turned out to be one of the waitresses—even spoke English. That she had learned to say what she did meant that this wasn't the first time she'd encountered what she considered inappropriate behavior. I don't know how she knew that this sailor didn't wash his hands after he went to the restroom; perhaps she knew of others. I was embarrassed for him, and I was embarrassed for myself. Not that I didn't wash my hands like he had failed to do, or was at least accused of failing to do, but that I was guilty by association. I wondered then if Japanese people viewed us Americans as somehow unclean. I guess sometimes you just have to swear like a sailor to make an impression on one!

Years later, I had an experience while dining in a restaurant. I went to the bathroom, and there was a well-dressed man in a nice suit standing next to me at another urinal. When he was through, he walked right out of the bathroom. When I returned to my table, after washing my hands thoroughly and using my elbow instead of my hand to push open the bathroom door, I noticed the same guy sitting a few tables away from my date and me. He was sitting with his family eating, and they were passing a basket of bread around the table. I had to look away. I also thought that this guy could easily run into an acquaintance and he would likely shake hands with that person. In our society it's considered rude not to shake someone's hand. In Japan, people bow and don't shake hands. I think some of that may have something to do with hygiene.

Hands are a very important in Japanese culture. I learned that many Japanese people base their assessment of how clean you are as a person on the cleanliness of your hands. I noticed while living there that many Japanese men got manicures, and their hands and nails were always clean and well cared for. Even a little bit of dirt underneath a nail revealed a lot about you. Working on a naval vessel, we frequently worked on machinery that relied on grease and oil, and it was easy to get your hands dirty and have some of that grime get under your nails. Before I went out in public, I was always careful to check my nails. Even today, though I no longer do that kind of manual labor, I'm still very conscious of the condition of my hands generally and my nails specifically.

I work in a business in which I have to meet and greet a lot of people, and just as I think of my appearance as a business card, I think of my hands as my résumé. When I extend my hand to shake someone else's, that's the first thing that comes in direct contact with them. They can both see and feel it. As a result, I pay close attention to the condition of my hands. I try not to judge other people on that basis, but I do notice the condition of their fingernails out of force of habit. Most of the time, I'm in the position where I am being judged worthy of doing work for these people, so my opinion of them doesn't really matter as much as their opinion of me. I'm not about to give anyone a reason to subtract from their estimation of me because of poorly cleaned hands.

While it isn't very popular for men here in the States, I did enjoy receiving manicures in Japan. They are much more accessible there—both less expensive and more inviting to men. I don't imagine that many of you reading this book, perhaps looking down on your poorly-cared-for nails, are eager to be seen ducking into the local nail salon. Maybe if you ever make it to Japan yourself, and I highly recommend you do, you'll see what I mean. In the meantime, it's very easy to care for your own nails as long as you take a little time and have the right equipment. Just as the Japanese judge others on how well kept their hands are, and I perceive it in my own life, you too will be judged by people looking at your hands. If your nails are too long or simply dirty, or your cuticles are torn or bloody, it's time to get your personal résumé—your nails—in order. And beyond the professional, when you are sitting across the table from a girl you want to impress on a first date, I promise you she's paying attention to what your hands look like. The cleaner and more attractive your hands, the better your chances she'll let them anywhere near her after dinner.

So let's get started. I've purchased a nice kit for doing the work. I think it's important to have the right tools for the right job. I haven't gone to the extreme and bought titanium or gold-plated nail clippers or anything, but I do have a manicure set that is nicer than the clippers you frequently see in a bowl or bin near the cashier at a drug store. I guess that maybe it's the barber in me (more on that later) that believes that any cutting instrument needs to be sharp and well made. Those less-than-a-dollar devices will work, but they grow dull too quickly, and before you know it, they are tearing up your nails and leaving jagged edges that make the job of filing them more difficult and time consuming.

Later on, we're going to talk more about treating yourself well, and a small extravagance like a decent manicure set isn't too much to do for yourself if you think you're valuable.

The Art of the Self-Manicure

Here's how I go about the task of trimming and cleaning my nails to make certain that I put my best hand forward:

1. Thoroughly wash your hands with warm water and a mild soap, preferably one that has some kind of lotion in it. Harsh deodorant soap like you might use on your body isn't the best thing to use here. Those soaps tend to dry your skin. I can remember commercials for a manly soap called Lava. It had pumice in it (essentially ground-up volcanic rock) that was supposed to help get rid of any kind of dirt or stains the most studly of men could get on their hands. Don't go to that extreme or to the opposite end of the spectrum with lavender-scented soap. If you have dirt under your nails you can either use a brush to scrub it out, or use the pointy end of the nail file to get underneath the nail to remove it.

2. Get a shallow bowl and pour in one-half to one inch of cuticle remover solution. (You can find this at most drug stores; some brands are Trind, Nutra Nail, and Sally Hansen.) Place your hand in the bowl so that your fingernails are completely submerged in the liquid.

3. Soak your hand for approximately five minutes.

4. Use the cuticle push-back tool to gently push the skin from the bottom of the nail down toward the knuckle. Most good manicure tool sets will have a cuticle pusher. Often they have round wooden handles like a tongue depressor. They will have a tip that is made of soft stone. It will be pointed like a spear on one side and flattened on the other. Use the flat side to rest on the nail as you push the cuticle back.

5. Use the cuticle scissors to trim the dead skin that you've pushed up. Cuticle scissors can look like this:

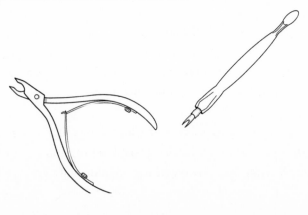

6. Once you're done with cuticle removal, you can use the clippers or trimmers to cut your nails. I believe that men should keep their nails fairly short. Regardless of the length, it is recommended that men trim their fingernails so that they are slightly rounded. Your nails should follow the shape of your fingertips and not be cut straight across or squared off.

7. The last step is to take a nail file and round off the sharp edge of the nail that trimming produced.

If you don't feel like tending to your cuticles (and not every guy chooses to take this step), at least make sure you maintain an appropriate length for your nails at all times.

I've never been a big fan of clear nail polish, though I know that some men do apply it (or have it applied) because it helps to protect nails from damage. I figure clean and neat is enough for me, and probably for you.

I also give my feet and toenails the same treatment, following the same steps. The only difference is that I cut my toenails straight across instead of following the curve. It is painful to have any part of your nail extend beyond the edge of the flesh of your toe. Having that nail driven into the tip of a shoe is really unpleasant. A lot of people don't think that much about their feet and their care and appearance. Out here in L.A., with the weather and the beaches, feet are on display a lot more than in other parts of the country. I can't tell you the number of nasty-looking feet I've seen in my time out here. If your hands are your résumé, then your feet are your references. You never know when they're going to be called on to vouch for you, so you'd better have them in good order. Every now and then I will soak my feet in water and Epsom salts. I'm lucky that I'm not on my feet all day like some people are, so I don't go all out when it comes to treating my feet well. But if you are working a job where you have to stand behind a counter all day, or you've been training for a marathon and your dogs are barking at the end of the day, soaking them this way can bring needed relief. When you wash your feet in the shower, make sure you clean between your toes with soap and water. Dry those places thoroughly with a towel afterward.

Making Yourself Presentable: Shaving

Along with never being taught how to tie a tie, no one ever showed me the proper way to shave. I've heard a lot of men say the same thing, and it seems strange that the primary hygienic and aesthetic task that most boys and men have to perform is essentially left to self-discovery. When you think about the fact that as adolescents we're given razors to drag across our faces with no clear instruction on just what to do, I'm even more surprised that shaving isn't given the same kind of respect as "the birds and the bees" conversation. Well, since most men I know never had that conversation with their fathers either, maybe it is. I can understand the potential for embarrassment in talking with your son about sex, but shaving? I suppose trial and error has worked for generations, but I know that in my case, I had some painful trials and a few too many errors in my effort to be clean shaven.

One of those experiments was with an electric razor. I know that some men swear by them and some men swear at them. I'm the latter. I used an electric razor briefly, figuring that it was more convenient because it was a relatively simple exercise. For some reason, my skin broke out terribly after coming into contact with the metal screens that cover the actual cutting blades. Even if I hadn't broken out, I don't think I would have liked the electric razor. There is something about the idea of standing and rubbing at my face repeatedly with a noisy electric motor in hand that is the opposite of soothing. I don't really even like the way electric razors look. Just as with the care of your nails, shaving involves the use of tools, and there are certain aesthetic elements to a tool—whether it is a carpenter's hammer, a surgeon's scalpel, a painter's brush, or a mason's trowel—that let you know that they "feel" right. For me, an electric razor never really felt right in my hand. Maybe it was because of my lack of appreciation for them that my skin reacted so badly to their touch.

As I intimated earlier, at one point during my time in the navy I became a ship's barber. As a result, I understand better than most the kind of precision that goes into a very close and injury-free shave. I like how clean and smooth my face feels after a shave, and I feel like I'm treating myself well when I give myself a good shave.

I know that a lot of men complain that the pace of daily life is so fast that they feel rushed to get everything done on any given day. I agree that for most of us, life is too full of appointments and deadlines, obligations and demands. However, in keeping with the theme of keeping yourself valuable, I believe it's important to recognize your worth by setting aside time to take care of yourself.

Another important aspect to shaving is its ritualistic place in our lives. Among the essentials of becoming a successful man (no matter what age you are), shaving is one of the more obvious signs of our transition from boyhood to adulthood. Since it is one of those markers, those milestones, those rites of passage, I think it should be treated like one. Along with the idea of using tools, how you approach shaving can either be meaningful or it can be just another task to check off of your "to do" list. I wish that I had learned these skills from my own foster father, and perhaps you are lucky enough to have learned them from your dad. Remember, when the time comes, you owe it to your son to teach him. But in case you have questions about how to get it done properly, I'll share my own experiences here. Why not use it as an opportunity to reflect on how far you've come and how you value yourself and your appearance as an individual of value?

My Personal Process

A lot of what you read about skin care suggests that you shower before you shave or even shave while showering. The idea is that the steam from the shower will soften your skin and hair follicles, making the razor's job easier and the irritation less. I don't normally follow either of those two excellent bits of advice, but that doesn't mean you shouldn't give them a try if irritation is a problem for you. You need two things to get the job done right and just how you get them is up to you to a certain extent: heat and moisture. I use a towel that I soak in the hottest water that comes out of the tap. I wring out the excess moisture and let the towel rest on my face for a couple of minutes. This reminds me of the Westerns I used to watch where men went to the town's barber to have their face shaven with a straight-edge razor. As much as it always seemed to bode poorly for whoever was getting shaven in the Westerns, I always find it comforting and relaxing. If you have a place in your bathroom where you can sit—on the toilet or the side of the tub—that's even better for chilling out as your face heats up. With a towel over your face and your eyes closed, it is much easier to shut out all the distractions and let the hundreds of thoughts that are usually racing through your mind exit through your opened pores.

After my hot towel treatment, I apply a little bit of shaving oil to my face. If you're not familiar with shaving oil, you should be. Like hot water or the towel, it helps to soften your beard, but it also applies an additional layer of protection and conditioning lubrication so that the hard steel of the blade glides more smoothly over your skin. I use the Lemon Essential pre-shave oil from The Art of Shaving, but you can find various shaving oils from places such as Bath and Body Works, American Crew, Pacific Shaving, and many other companies. A quick Google search will turn up lots of options and vendors, or simply ask at your local drugstore or department store. Next, I mix up a batch of shaving cream. That's right, I use a special shaving mug, a bit of powder and water, and a brush to whip up a froth of cream that I then apply to my face. I don't use a gel product—the oil and cream together provide the same face-saving effects as a good gel. Among the brands of shaving powder available are Remington, Williams, Magic, Royal Crown, and Magic Skin. I generally look for products that include aloe to soothe and moisturize the skin. Some even have a sun protection factor (SPF) rating to help keep the sun's ultraviolet rays from doing damage to your skin.

My face is steamed, I have my shaving oil on as a base, topped by a nice coat of freshly made shaving cream. It could be a drag, but to me this is one of the highlights of manhood. I begin to shave, being careful to always take long smooth strokes with the grain of my beard. I've seen men shave themselves with short choppy motions going over and over the same area. That's just a recipe for razor burn, as is going against the grain of your beard. For most of us, our hair grows out and down. Shave with downward strokes. Generally, if I have a relatively new blade, it only takes one pass to get all the hair. That's one advantage of the preparation. Your skin is exposed to the sharp cutting edge of the blade for as little time as possible. Also, don't press down hard with the razor. A light touch is always best. Too much pressure also irritates the skin.

For African American men, going with the grain of facial hair is particularly important. This is one of the ways to prevent or lessen razor bumps. Early on, I knew that I did not want to get razor bumps. I saw friends and fellow sailors who had them, and an alternative shaving product for them was a product called Magic Shave. I'm sure it is fine for some folks, but I never wanted to use it myself. A razorless method for removing facial hair, it works on a chemical basis. No matter how it's explained to me, what I hear in my head is *That stuff burns the hair off my face.* That may not be the precise chemical explanation for what happens, but how else could it be that the hair disappears? It works great for those that need it and like it, but for me, no thanks. Or you could always grow a beard, and sometimes that's the solution—just not in the armed services.

Once you've gone over your entire face one time, with the grain, you can go back over it (after relathering) across or against the grain, if you choose to. When you shave, use cold water to rinse the razor as necessary. When you're done shaving, it's a good idea to rinse your face once again with hot water. I then apply aftershave lotion or moisturizer. Always look for a product that doesn't contain alcohol. You're not looking for some sexy scented product, you're looking for something that will help your skin recover from the trauma of having a sharp piece of metal dragged across it.

A moisturizer does exactly what its name implies. You'll likely find that over time and as you continue to follow this regimen, you'll have far less irritation than you did when you first started out. A lot of men today shave their heads or a portion of their head, and the same guidelines apply to your scalp as to your face.

If my barbershop-style process is too much—especially for the daily grind—just remember the essentials every time you shave: use a clean, well-maintained blade (and I don't care if there are two, three, or ten blades; whatever feels good to you); moisten and warm your face before shaving, even if it's just a few splashes of hot water; apply a shave oil if possible but always a shaving cream or gel; shave with the grain; rinse and apply a postshave ointment. Now you look great.

For men who keep a beard or facial hair like a moustache or goatee, just be sure that you have a good set of clippers and that you keep your facial hair well maintained. Although I sometimes use a straight razor because of my experience as a barber, I would recommend that you use clippers or a regular razor to maintain the lines between facial hair and skin. If you are wondering if facial hair is appropriate at your job, look at what other men farther up the ladder are doing. If some of them sport facial hair, you are probably okay. If not, it might be time to think about losing it.

Again, I want to stress that approaching this time as a ritual of manhood is important. Most of the time, we shave because we have to: I'm going out on a date, have to shave. I have to go to work, must shave. My wife doesn't like the feel of my scruffy skin against hers, better shave. As a result of all those haves, musts, and betters, we look at it as a task and not as something we're doing for ourselves. That's okay, and you may not want to go through the process I've outlined every time you shave. I think that setting aside time on the weekend to care for your nails and have a proper, ritualized shave—when you aren't doing it to meet any kind of obligation—is a good idea. That is time you are setting aside for your personal upkeep, so that when you head back to school or the office on Monday, you're feeling confident that your calling card, résumé, and references are all in good order. Another thing that rituals do is to remind us of something important in our lives. You started to shave at roughly the same time as you refined many of the dreams that you had about the shape that you wanted your life to take. These weren't merely childhood fantasies, but real plans when you began to take greater control of your life.

In boot camp, if someone wasn't properly shaved, the penalty was a dry shave, using a razor but no water and no shaving cream. At one time or another we've all probably had to dry shave, so you know how unpleasant that can be. In the navy, there are consequences for everything. We talked about everything being checked on the ship from bow to stern (from the front of the ship all the way to the rear). If you are going out anywhere, it makes sense to check yourself from one end to the other to be certain you are squared away.

I do most of my upkeep myself these days, but finding a good local barber is also essential to your profile, so ask around and find someone you like. There are a lot of high-end places that will charge you a lot of money, but there are also a lot of places that are quite affordable. The key is finding someone you like and maintaining a relationship. Depending on the length of your hair and the style, you should visit the barber anywhere from every few weeks for closely clipped hair to every few months for that layered look. Hey, if you're bald, think of all the money you save. Whatever you do, don't ever do the comb-over or the fluff-over as you grow older. It will look strange to everyone though they won't say anything—at least not to you.

Now that you've read this chapter, go look in the mirror. Is nose hair sprouting where it shouldn't be? Are your nails claws? How can you improve the way you look and feel about yourself so that you make the best impression on others? Get your clean on, my brother.

CHAPTER FOUR

FROM THE OUTSIDE IN: PUTTING YOUR BEST FOOT FORWARD

The other day, my wife, LaNette, and I took our two daughters, Indigo and Azure to the shoe store. Indigo needed a pair of casual walking-around shoes. Los Angeles is a pretty fashion-conscious place, but LaNette and I made a decision early on that we weren't going to let our daughters get caught up in that. Every parent has to deal with the keeping-up-with-the-Joneses phenomenon, but out here, the Joneses live in an eight-bedroom, 6,000-square-foot home with a pool, a tennis court, and a gated security entrance that only lets you imagine what splendors lie on the other side. I don't begrudge anybody for their success or make judgments about how they choose to spend their money, but LaNette and I believe that indulging your kids in extravagance early in life will only lead to problems down the road.

Thanks to the Internet and shows like *TMZ*, we all know what can happen to spoiled kids. These days, you hear about all this stuff whether you want to or not, but at least it makes an impression that having it all isn't necessarily as great as it seems.

We walked into an athletic shoe store and together checked out the section where the old-school Converse Chuck Taylors were on display. As a kid, it seemed like just about everyone was wearing Chuck Taylors. They were no big deal, just a basic sneaker that you wore until the canvas uppers were tattered and the soles were as porous as a sponge. They've gone in and out of fashion over the years, showing up everywhere from school kids to punk rockers. Like everything else, they've been co-opted by fashion as well, showing up with outrageous designs or luxury materials. But I'll always have a place in my heart for the basic white or black Chuck Taylors and their simple, useful style.

Too Much!

Just before our shopping excursion, I'd seen a piece on MTV about an artist who painted custom-made shoes for hip-hop artists. He was charging $3,000 *a shoe* to create a one of a kind look. Six thousand dollars a pair! I was impressed by his talent and ingenuity. I'd been interested in art my whole life and I never even considered that I could make a more than decent wage painting someone's shoes. Well, you know what happened next. Kids saw those shoes being worn by a few hip-hop celebrities and wanted to be like them. They knew they couldn't afford those shoes. Societal pressure and advertisements convinced some people that they *had to* have them. A need is born every minute. Where there's a need, there's always someone willing to meet it, so Nike introduced a line of shoes perhaps inspired by this guy. I knew that sneakers meant a whole lot to some people, and I'd heard stories of Nike fanatics lining up outside a particular store when a new version of a shoe was going to be released. My reaction was usually this: Please! Can you be so desperate to find some way to think of yourself as having value that being one of the first to buy a new pair of sneakers is going to have you waiting in line all morning? Don't you have a job to go to? A family? A life?

Compared to the Chuck Taylors we used to have, we can all express ourselves in countless ways through the kinds of sneakers or shoes we wear. I think it's great to have some fun with what you put on your feet. But it seems to me that some of us take it too far and put too much emphasis on the latest, the neatest, the coolest. And wherever kids (or adults, for that matter) are willing to spend money, there are going to be manufacturers and marketers more than happy to meet that demand. I think that if you let the brand of sneaker you wear determine whether or not you feel of value, then you actually run the risk of devaluing yourself and having others do the same to you. And if someone's artistic expression is through painting sneakers, or ties, or T-shirts, that's great. Why not let our art touch everything? But we also have to be aware that some big companies want us to want those things so that they can make their annual budgets.

Staying Grounded

As I was standing in that store with my family, I was thinking about my brief exploration of the sneaker subculture. What I'd stumbled across was probably an exception to the rule. Most people wouldn't put that much value on a pair of shoes. And as much as I believe that people should determine their value from the inside out, I know that we don't always do that. I was willing to just forget about the whole issue of shoes and value and our culture, pay for my daughter's shoes and then get out of there.

We were standing in line waiting to pay when we noticed the woman in front of us. She was pushing a baby in a stroller. The child couldn't have been more than five or six months old and since he or she was mostly covered by a blanket and all I could see was a brief glimpse of balled fists and a bit of wrinkled forehead and a gummy yawn, it wasn't easy to identify the gender of the infant. The woman handed the clerk a small shoe box. The cashier scanned it, and the numbers came up on the register: $78. I remembered the cartoons I watched as a kid and hoped that my eyes didn't bug out and then snap back into their sockets. I felt like they might have. LaNette and I exchanged a raised eyebrow. Seventy-eight dollars for a pair of shoes for an infant who wasn't even capable of walking yet? Seventy-eight dollars for a pair of shoes that child will outgrow before the week is out?

Okay, that's not for us, and that's fine for that woman, but I hoped that those shoes, and the ones she was wearing, had enough traction to keep them both from sliding down the slippery slope of indulgence.

I feel a bit hypocritical sharing this story. After all, what you're about to read has to do with clothes and fashion. I'm a big believer in having shoes that complete an outfit. I can remember many times when I saw a man walking down the street or sitting in a meeting and I was really impressed with his style of dress. But then I'd see his shoes and they were a fashion tragedy. I like shoes and I like having nice shoes. I don't spend thousands of dollars on them, but I do believe that paying attention to your shoes and finding appropriate shoes for the right occasion and what they say about you is important.

Your Shoes Send a Message

Just as your hands and your face are your calling card, you need to think about the message that your footwear sends. We'll talk later about picking the right suit, pants, and shirts, but right now I'm building you from the ground up. In my opinion, someone who really has a sense of style pays attention to their shoes. There's a reason why we use the expression "putting your best foot forward" or describe someone as "well-heeled" when we mean they are wealthy.

When it comes to all things fashion, I don't believe in chasing trends. That probably doesn't surprise you now that you know I won't pay $6,000 for a pair of artistic sneakers. For dress shoes, I wear a pair of classic Ferragamo lace-ups. They are timeless. You can go back to photographs of men in the 1950s, and see shoes almost identical to what I wear today. Ferragamos are, by some standards, expensive shoes, but they are made of high-quality materials and if well cared for, will last for many years. I may not think it valuable to spend money on trendy sneakers, but I do find value in having good, high-quality, classically designed dress shoes that I won't be looking to replace when next season's fashions are introduced.

Shoe Care

You can spend as much or about as little as you want on your dress shoes, but what I learned is that caring for them matters a whole lot more than what you paid for them. Just as I was able to use an iron to make whatever clothes I had more presentable, you can do the same thing with the tools available to care for your shoes.

You know those men that I described earlier with the terrible footwear? The cause of the tragedy wasn't always that they wore the wrong kind of shoe or that they wore shoes of inferior quality—most often it was that they didn't take proper care of their shoes. Part of our routine in the navy was polishing our shoes. I don't think it is a lost art, but I have friends who were required to polish their shoes weekly as kids, and now seldom do it as adults. Kind of strange to see that habit die out. You'd think that if you were paying for something as an adult that impacts how other people see you, you'd be more and not less diligent about taking care of it.

In a recent article in *Essence* magazine, Kwame Jackson, who earned notoriety on the reality TV show *The Apprentice*, and who did not win but was later selected by the business mogul Donald Trump to head a project, was asked about his fashion tips for the successful businessman. Guess what? Among those on his list was polishing your shoes. He also pointed out that women often notice a man's shoes and put a great deal of emphasis on them when assessing someone's suitability. So, it's not just this sailor who thinks that shining shoes is important.

You're about to enroll in Shoe Care 101. Here are the materials you're going to need. A typical shoeshine kit includes:

- A shoeshine and polish brush
- Shine or buffing cloths (chamois)
- A shoehorn
- Standard brown and black polish
- An all-purpose leather cleaner and conditioner

When should you polish your shoes? Depending upon how much use they get, a weekly, biweekly, or monthly shine will be needed.

How should you store your shoes when you're not wearing them? A lot of people believe in using shoe trees. They help to keep air circulating inside the shoe and they help them hold their form. That keeps the leather in good shape. Water is leather's natural enemy, so if you've come in out of the rain and your feet are soaked, there are a couple of things that you can do to extend the life of your shoes. Wipe them clean and dry as much as possible. If you're coming in from slush or snow, get any street salt off your shoes, as salt will destroy the leather over time. You can pack wet shoes with balled-up newspaper to help draw out the moisture and maintain shape. Then don't wear them again until they are completely dried out—for your sake as much as the shoes.

How to Polish Shoes

Step 1: Workspace

Shoe polish is a disaster if it gets where it shouldn't be. Take the time to cover your work area with an old rag or newspapers in order to prevent polish stains. Also, try to be careful throughout your shine job. If you don't want to get polish on your hands, a pair of latex gloves does the trick.

Step 2: Start on a clean slate

Before applying polish, make sure your shoes are clean. Give your shoes a once over with a shoeshine brush or chamois or cotton cloth.

Step 3: Polish

A note on polish: Shoe polish comes in three forms: liquid, cream, and paste. Which one you use is a matter of personal choice. The important thing to keep in mind is that they all contain chemicals which can be harmful if you're exposed to them for a long time. Wearing those latex gloves can lessen your exposure. They also come in various sheens: gloss, high gloss, and parade gloss. Depending upon how much shine you want, and what the original finish on the shoes was, you'll use one of those three.

With shoe in hand, apply a sufficient amount of polish with your shoe polish brush. Spread it evenly over the entire upper of the shoe. For hard-to-reach areas, you can use a cotton swab or toothbrush, but don't drive yourself crazy over every nook and cranny of the shoe. Wait 15 to 20 minutes for the polish to dry.

Step 4: Back to work

Once your shoe is dry, use the shoeshine brush to wipe off the polish. Again, use a clean cotton swab or toothbrush for those hard-to-reach spots.

Step 5: The finishing touch

Every step of the shoeshine process is important, but if your buff job is subpar, you are not going to be happy with the end result. Use a clean, lint-free shine cloth or chamois to give your shoes the shine they deserve. Rub vigorously, alternating between a back and forth and circular motion to ensure that you cover the entire surface. Turn your buffing cloth frequently to be certain that you aren't spreading half-dried polish from one area to the next. That's all there is to it.

As I mentioned when talking about shaving and other aspects of personal grooming, turning this into a kind of ritual is important. Take your time. Listen to some favorite music. Treating your belongings with the same care that you treat yourself is a way of reinforcing the idea that you are valuable.

Don't be afraid to ask a sales clerk what the proper care of your shoes should be when you buy them, and chances are the store will be happy to sell you the right equipment. You can also order accessories at online retailers such as Zappos.com. Take good care of your shoes and you will save money, look better, and, if your shoes hold up, feel better.

Taking a Shine to Your Shoes: The Shoe Shine Shop

Depending on where you live and what your job schedule is like, you're not always going to have the time to shine your shoes yourself. You can always pay to have them shined by someone else. This may not be possible for many people because shoe repair shops and shoe shine stands are a disappearing part of Main Street America. Dropping off a pair of shoes to be repaired or polished is a pretty straightforward process, but getting them shined at a stand by someone else while you're still wearing them can be a little intimidating the first time you do it. I prefer to do things myself, but I know some people who really like the idea of having them shined by someone else.

Let's say you are traveling for business and you discover that your shoes were scuffed on the trip. You didn't bring a shoeshine kit with you (always try to bring at least a polishing rag when you travel for business; some hotels offer them free to guests) and you are going directly from the airport to the meeting. There's a shoeshine stand in the airport, so you stop there. The price of a shine varies from place to place, and keep in mind that the person doing the work may not own the spot. They might simply be getting paid minimum wage or worse, so the main question is how much to tip them for their service. Generally, when it comes to tipping in restaurants, the twenty percent rule comes into play—you tip at least fifteen percent of the total bill, and twenty percent is considered a generous tip for good service. That's not true with other people who provide services, like shoe shiners, so somewhere between two or three dollars is appropriate even if the shine itself only cost five dollars.

These days, parking valets, shoe shiners, barbers, and nearly everyone else who provides a service expect and deserve a tip. It's not a bad idea to have a few dollar bills in your pocket when you know you are on the go. Casually pulling a bill out of your breast pocket and draping it over your shoulder isn't necessary. Handing it directly to the person and looking him or her in the eye and saying thank you is enough. You're not trying to draw attention to yourself or your kind gesture. Now is not the time to be flamboyant but respectful and grateful. Think about putting yourself in that person's shoes and you'll adopt the right attitude. And even better, your shoes look as good as new and you make a favorable impression as you enter your meeting to make the sale, clinch the deal, or speak to new colleagues on behalf of your company.

A Shoe-In to Succeed: The Basic Types of Shoes

Now that you are committed to taking good care of your nice new shoes, here's an overview of the common types of men's shoes. It's important to find a shoe in which you feel comfortable, but some shoes are generally better with certain outfits.

The Oxford Dress Shoe

Some fashion experts consider these the classic. Oxfords have round toes, sometimes with a cap, and closed lacing. Oxfords are a perfect option for business wear, and when there is no cap on the toe, can do double duty as formal shoes as long as they are well polished. Oxfords with broguing along the cap's edge, or trimming along the uppers, are still fine for a suit; full brogues are more appropriate with more casual pant and shirt outfits.

The Wing Tip Dress Shoe

The wing tip, with a brogued cap (an extra piece of patterned leather sewn over the toe of the shoe) coming to a point at the center of the top curving back and down along the sides, is suit level in black and business casual in brown. They are bit flashier than the other classics, and may call attention to themselves. This is not necessarily a bad thing, of course, but as a result you probably don't want to wear them as frequently. You could get away with wearing

the same oxfords three or four times a week without anyone knowing, but if you did that with these more detailed shoes, you'd probably end up being known as the wing-tip guy. Wing tips have been
co-opted into more casual styles, so don't pick up a style that looks
like it is part combat boot–part dress shoe and expect to wear it with
a suit. Again, feel free to start a dialog with the shoe salesman about
whether a style is right for your purposes.

The Derby and the Blucher

The derby is similar in shape to the oxford, but bears open lacing. It
is still appropriate to wear with a suit, and goes with a khakis-and-
blazer look more naturally than oxfords. The blucher is a slightly
sleeker open-laced shoe of similar versatility. Plain-toed or with a
brogued cap like the wing tip, these dress shoes will match a suit in
formality; with more decoration they carry a blazer well. In suede
rather than smooth leather, these are among the best shoes to wear
with jeans or khakis.

Boots

Dress boots bring some ruggedness to dress footwear, making them
a worthy option in the winter. In addition, their slip on and off
feature, along with superior comfort, make them a favorite among
travelers and those not requiring the formality of the oxford.

The Loafer and the Monk Strap

Slip-on shoes are casual by nature. Those appropriate for business
casual wear include bit loafers, with a metal link across the middle;
monk straps, with a buckle closure; and penny loafers, with a slotted
leather band across the top. Tassel loafers, which are exactly what

they sound like, are accepted as business formal in some circles while relegated to weekend wear in others.

White Bucks

White bucks are oxfords made of white buckskin, a rough leather that isn't really white. Usually, you would wear them with a seersucker suit or other summer fabrics like tan gabardine and white linen, and generally, only in the summer. A variation on these are saddle shoes: they have a brown leather saddle-shaped patch extending over the middle of the shoe. The patch can come in various sizes. Some people really like multicolored shoes, but I'm not a fan.

PARTS OF A SHOE

Aglet	the metal or plastic part at the end of a shoelace
Cap	an additional bit of leather added to the toe
Cuff	the upper ridge around the back of the shoe
Eyelet	the hole through which the lace is threaded
Eyelet tab	a reinforced leather or fabric where the eyelets are punched
Heel	the flat section on the bottom of the shoe at the rear
Insole	the padded fabric inside the shoe
Instep	covers the foot
Shank	the narrow part of the sole under the instep
Sole	the bottom supporting part of the shoe
Upper	the top part of the shoe above the sole
Vamp	the part of the shoe covering the instep
Welt	the strip between the sole and upper

Sock It to Me: The Role of Socks

What good are shoes without socks? I'm pretty conservative when it comes to these as well. I prefer solid colors—black, navy, gray—with black shoes. Brown shoes take a lighter color like beige or green. I know that some men who work in corporate America and are bound by certain rules governing how they dress like to rebel a little with a flair of color in their socks, including argyle (a diamond-shaped pattern) or more flamboyant colors or patterns. That is a matter of preference as well, but the principle of drawing too much attention to yourself comes into play. Maybe you do want to stand out and be known as the guy who wears fire-engine-red socks all the time. That's a risk you have to take, so just be aware that when you make a conscious choice to stand out, some people may applaud you while others boo you. You don't have to conform to everything that society says, but you should be aware of the consequences (good and bad) for choosing to go your own way. As long as you're putting your best foot forward and making the statement about yourself that you intend to make, as far as I'm concerned nearly everything goes in footwear and other aspects of fashion as well.

Now, your feet look great in those classy shoes and socks. But why are you standing there naked? It's time to talk about clothes.

CHAPTER FIVE

CLOTHES MAKE THE MAN

The title of this chapter is somewhat ironic. I hope you get that, after everything I've written about viewing yourself as valuable and working from the inside out. That said, clothes and your appearance are essential to your success as a man. I wish that I could say that all people will reserve judgment until they get to know your personality, your temperament, your values, and your beliefs. That doesn't happen very often. Most people won't even give you the opportunity to express your inner self unless the outer self fits the bill. What exactly that means varies from person to person, but for the most part what I've said about your hands, face, and shoes still applies. Exactly what style of clothes you wear can matter less than the impression that your outfit was put together in a thoughtful way and your clothes are well maintained. If you are dressed in clean and neat looking clothes—whether they are the baggiest of jeans and an oversized T-shirt or a pair of khaki pants and a T-shirt—stain-free, unwrinkled, pleasant-smelling clothes are what really matters. I'm sure that by this point in the book I no longer need to add that baggy pants and a T-shirt for a job interview rarely fly, as much as khakis and bluchers to a date on the beach will get you nowhere.

Say That I Don't Know What's Crackin' . . .

I'll admit up front that I'm not a big fan of most of the hip-hop look that many young people wear today. I'm sorry—call me old-fashioned, out of touch, or whatever, but ever since the oversized-baggy-pants, show-your-boxers/briefs/butt-crack look came into vogue, I've felt bad for kids. Seeing young men walking around with their belts below their crotches, their wide-legged pants dragging through the city's grit and grime, their baseball caps all askew, makes this navy veteran cringe. I know that it's a look, that it's an affectation, an imitation of popular music stars and all that, but it is the very opposite of what I and many other people consider squared away.

To me, squared away means that what you are wearing conforms to the usual and accepted standards. Those standards mean clothes that fit. In other words, your clothes conform to the shape and size of your body. The hip-hop look annoys me because I just don't get what is so great about looking sloppy. But when I see a young man wearing oversized pants and shirt, if they are freshly ironed and neatly creased and obviously clean and well cared for, they earn a pass from me. I may not like the look, and would never adopt it for myself, but at least they care about their clothes.

Beware and Be Aware of the Messages Your Clothes Send

Another reason why I object to the hip-hop style is that I've read and I believe that it celebrates the thug life to a certain extent. When I worked as a corrections officer, I saw prisoners come into the system. They had to give up their personal clothes and were issued a prison uniform. That meant a pair of khaki pants and a khaki shirt along with socks and underclothes. Prisoners didn't get to spend a lot of time selecting what items they wanted—they were given whatever was on hand and in a size that was close to what they needed. Oftentimes belts were neither available nor issued for a variety of reasons; consequently prisoners didn't have anything to hold up their pants. As a result, a lot of them walked around with baggy, saggy pants and took up the look as a preference. It's not surprising that once released from prison they took this style out onto the streets with them and somewhere along the line it merged into hip-hop culture. After working at a prison for three years, I can certainly tell you that there is nothing that I would celebrate or take away from prison life and use in my life of freedom and hope—especially not sagging baggy pants. What you are saying about yourself when you wear clothes of that style is not a message you want to send. Having lived on those mean streets and having seen friends die violent deaths, I don't see much to celebrate. Maybe even more disturbing is the emphasis on oversized clothes. It signals a lack of self-esteem and self-value. Oversized clothes say "I want to be big and important, but I'm not, so I'm going to put on this uniform that helps me take up more space." Is that the message you want to send?

If you really value yourself, you don't need to put on a display of being big. You are big because you believe in yourself and your abilities. You matter because of who you are, and you don't have to draw attention to yourself with your bling or your bigness. You want people to notice you and admire you because of who you are as a person and not as a purchaser.

Clothes send a message, and you need to be sure that it coincides with what you think, believe, and hope is true about yourself. Clothes don't make the man, but you do make the choices about what to wear and how to wear it. We go through our early life having most of these choices made for us, usually by mom. Sometimes she would drag you to the store and make you try on a bunch of stuff. Even worse, everyone's least favorite Christmas gift was clothes from Aunt Dorothy and Uncle Jess. As we mature, we are given the opportunity to take control of these decisions, and that's an important power to have. We owe it to our parents to walk out the door looking presentable and to show we understand the ways of the world by dressing appropriately for a job and succeeding when we are finally out in the world. As I said earlier, I've seen what happens to kids who don't succeed. If we are given the choice to control our destinies or not, do I even have to ask the question how would you choose to present yourself in public?

Check This Out

While I'm not a fan of the way hip-hop shows up on the streets, certain musicians really have eclectic styles that are fun to look at and might even lead to a few ideas. If you pick the right role models, they can help you figure out what your own style is. Kanye West has a real look and there are Web sites devoted to following his fashion. Sean Combs has been successful with his line, Sean John. There are many magazines devoted to the way men dress and carry themselves socially, and these can also be a great resource. Magazine subscriptions are relatively inexpensive, but you can also check them out online or at your local library. They usually tell you what brand of clothing they are profiling and what the costs are. These include: *GQ, Esquire, Details, Men's Journal,* and *Men's Health.* There is a great tradition of men subscribing to these magazines, so don't be afraid to add your name.

The Limits of My Advice

The title of this book is *A Boy Should Know How to Tie a Tie: And Other Lessons for Succeeding in Life*. We wear a tie at many of the important milestones, whether it's the celebration of a wedding or the mourning of a funeral. Those are the significant events in our lives. As you know, I didn't have a father to teach me how to get myself ready for those important markers in my advance toward manhood. Most of what we wear day-to-day, we pick up from our friends at school, our favorite musicians or movie stars, or a combination of those influences. Even if my dad had been around, how many kids stop to listen on their way out the door to play ball or hang with friends. But I was never offered help on the bigger stuff, so I decided that would be more of my focus in this book when it came to dress. It might be a little less fun, but it is the stuff that makes us men and we are all in it together on that journey.

On those times as a boy when I needed to elevate myself from my everyday life, I felt my father's absence most acutely. I could figure out how to get along in the neighborhood, but when it came to really rise above, I was lost. I don't want you to be lost, and so I offer you this bit of guidance. Take it as it's intended, as one man's view of what is right and proper.

Looking Good

The same way I gravitate toward a classic look in my choice of shoes, I definitely have that inclination when it comes to dressing nicely. When I think about dressing "nicely" I'm thinking about how to dress for work, a dinner date, or a more formal event like a graduation ceremony. As I said earlier, I'm going to leave what you wear on weekends to you, as long as you remember to keep your clothes in good condition and your pants covering your butt and secured with a belt. Unless you have a career in sports, I'll trust that you won't think a tracksuit passes as an actual outfit, no matter what you are doing.

As a writer, I'm very sensitive to language, and when I use the term "getting dressed up" I put the emphasis on the word "up." The idea is to put your best foot forward, to show yourself as the best that you are, your most valued self. That's especially true when it comes to going to work or to school. Ask yourself what your employer or your teachers would think of you and your clothing. I take a similar attitude: What you do on your time is basically up to you, but when its work time I expect you to dress appropriately. I don't expect you to wear a suit to school, but if you are in college and a professor has invited you to a social event after class—maybe an author is visiting your school—then I think a jacket with slacks and dress shoes is the appropriate attire. When your professor sees you arrive looking like you will positively represent your school, then you will be asked to such events again. This is one way to meet important people out in the world, and to a certain extent, it begins with the clothes.

By now, you can probably guess that a lot of what I have to say has to do with looking neat and clean and keeping your clothes the same way. I'm going to spend some time focusing on how to maintain what you have as well as on what you should have in your closet. Let's start with the basics.

A Suitable Option

For professional outings—meetings, lunches, conferences, interviews, and such—I always wear what I refer to as my uniform. I own three high-quality suits: one two-button and two three-button. They are all either wool or a wool blend. You may think that because

I live in California, a wool suit would be much too warm, but that's not the case. There are various types of wool. They are generally referred to by weight, and a summer-weight wool suit serves me well. I don't like polyester in most clothing—I prefer natural fibers—but I especially don't like it in suits. It has a kind of sheen and texture to it that makes a suit look and feel cheap and kind of tacky. Cotton suits are fine; they are lightweight and have a nice feel to them, but they can strike a more casual note, especially when worn without a tie. Cotton and linen suits also wrinkle more easily and show the wrinkles more obviously than wool. The good news is that there is a wide variety of quality suits available at different price points. You just need to take a little time to find what's right for you.

I have one black suit, one navy blue suit, and one gray suit. Brown would be okay too but it's not a color that looks good on many people. The suits' jackets are traditionally cut, and the pants are plain front, which is the more popular style these days. Pleated pants are okay, but to me they just add extra fabric and I find myself fussing with them too much. Pleats will also bulk out your appearance a little, so plain fronts help with a slimmer look.

My goal in choosing an outfit isn't to impress people, nor is it to blend in completely. I want my clothes to serve me and not me to serve them. I can't expect to go into a meeting with a producer and have a script approved on the basis of how good I'm looking that day. Instead, I have to be comfortable enough with my appearance that I can forget about it completely and make the best pitch for my material that I can. And I don't want to walk into a room with something so out of place that all anyone in the room thinks about is whether I'm color blind or something.

Another reason why I wear my uniform is that it's cost effective. Three classically tailored suits that won't go out of style should last ten years minimum if well cared for. They don't need to replaced for fashion reasons. Men have been wearing these suits for decades so I don't have to worry about wearing last year's color.

Why a "Uniform"?

I know that the idea of wearing a uniform or even calling my professional wardrobe that might be unappealing. The word elicits the perception that everyone should be alike in appearance. It's true the word "uniform" does mean even, equal, and the same. The military uses uniforms for practical reasons, but also to promote a sense of unity and pride. I know that whenever I wore my navy uniform, especially my blue dress uniform, I felt a sense of achievement and belonging. That didn't mean that I gave up my individuality. Too often, especially when we're young, we strive so hard to differentiate ourselves from our parents, from others, that we forget that there is a strength in numbers, and that belonging to something doesn't mean that we have to surrender ourselves completely. Conforming to rules and regulations doesn't mean that you've sold out and now you're part of some machine.

Maybe I refer to my dress clothes as my uniform because for most of my adult life I wore a uniform—first as a sailor, then as a prison guard, and later as a security guard. For pragmatic reasons, I liked having a uniform to wear. It cut down on the amount of thought I had to give each day to the question, *What am I going to wear?* I took comfort in knowing that when I went to work, I'd have something I could count on. You don't have to think of your wardrobe as a uniform the way I do, but it's good to have some basics as the foundation of your wardrobe that will work year after year, that you are comfortable with, but that you can also expand on depending on your mood or activity.

The Message I Want to Send

We spend a lot of our youth chasing trends. One year it's Levis, the next it's a hot European designer or some European influence. How many young men spent the nineties wearing velour jogging suits because of Russell Simmons? It's great for clothing makers because we're rushing out every six months for the new thing, but it can get a little exhausting and certainly pricey.

As a young person, you may not know exactly who you are. You're going to have to try on identities just like you will various clothes. One week, you're a rock star, the next an aspiring hip-hop star, the next a preppy . . . you get the idea. All those looks are out there for you to try on. That's fine. I had to do the same thing, but benefit from my experience and know that at some point you will have to stop all that identity swapping and settle more firmly into who you are for longer periods than this season's hot-ticket item. It's good to know that there are consistent styles you can call on and use to your benefit that will help you project the real you to the world at large. When you settle into a job, or even at school, it's helpful to project one identity and not be someone who is constantly, visibly trying to reinvent himself.

Dress for Success: What Does That Mean?

I have my uniform. It works for me in a variety of settings, and I can pull one out of the closet without having to think about it too much. It used to be that if you were going to work in an office, you could count on wearing a suit most of the time. Certainly, you'd be wearing a tie. Just look back at a photo of a business meeting taking place in 1950 and you'll see what I'm talking about. But the reality is that much of today's business has become somewhat more casual—to what degree depends on the business. Law firms still evoke a suit-and-tie mentality, maybe because some of the lawyers might have to show up in court on any given day. Banks too, though you see many tellers wearing a nice pair of slacks and a dress shirt. The best way to gauge what to wear to work is to start with the person who hired you for the job (if it's a man—I don't want you wearing skirts to work), and what other men on up the chain wear. It's always better to err on the side of formal for an interview and wear a suit even if the guy across the table is tieless. And you can always ask a boss as you get started. Sometimes a more casual dresser wants someone a little snappier working for them as a power play. I've added some general information about how to dress for this new office environment at the end of the chapter.

Additional Suit Concerns

Life in a suit would be boring if you only wore solid-colored fabrics. Depending on your build, patterns can help offset any issues you may think you have with your physique. Pin stripes in a suit fabric, especially very thin ones of a subtle color, can look really great and make you seem taller and thinner. You don't want a suit with stripes that makes you look like you stepped out of a prison film from the silent-movie era. Use the distance rule of thumb: if you can easily spot the pattern in a suit from more than thirty feet away, you're likely targeting yourself for gaudy comments—not about how good you look, but about how gaudy your suit is.

Another decision you have to make about a suit is whether you want to go with a single- or double-breasted jacket. Again, I don't believe in absolute rules, but you do want to look good. A double-breasted jacket has more fabric and a second set of buttons on the front. Because of that extra fabric, a relatively thin man can look like he's drowning in fabric even if the jacket is the right size. That's not a good look. Shorter men won't find a friend in the double-breasted jacket, either. That extra fabric makes them look even shorter. If you have the right build, a double-breasted suit can look great. It is more formal than a single-breasted, and shouldn't really be worn without a dress shirt and tie. David Letterman almost exclusively wears double-breasted jackets and he knows how to make them look good. The other thing about double-breasted jackets is that they look silly when unbuttoned. With a single-breasted jacket, you can get away with a tieless look, and buttoning and unbuttoning it is no problem in terms of ease or appearance.

With the two- or three-button suit, you need to keep in mind how many buttons to button on the jacket when you are standing. The rule of thumb is that you always have two buttons done up. Even if you have a four-button suit, you can get away with keeping the middle two buttons done and the top and bottom undone. So with the three-button suit, button the top two and let the third one stay open.

As you can see, even with the "uniform," you do have other things to think about. There's no such thing as thoughtless dressing, but the level of thought you put into the details pays off by expressing your personal style.

Adding Your Own Touch to the Uniform

Once you've established what some of your basic pieces are going to be, whether you are going to follow my lead and stick with suits or think a more casual approach is better, let's look at some of the other building blocks of a good wardrobe.

Dress Shirts 101: A Beginner's Guide

I like 100 percent cotton over any other fabric or blend. Cotton just feels good against my skin.

Dress shirts come in various styles. First, let's take a look at the types of dress shirts there are. One possible point of confusion is that some people refer to all men's dress shirts as "button-down" or "button-up" shirts. They are referring to the fact that these shirts have a row of buttons running up the front. The confusion occurs because shirt makers and retailers classify the style of dress shirts by their collars. One of those collars is a button-down collar: the ends or points of the collar have buttonholes in them that hold those ends down with buttons attached to the shirtfront. If you were to go into a store and ask for a button-down shirt, that's likely what you'd be shown: a shirt with a button-down collar. That may not be the type of shirt you want or that suits whatever use you've got in mind. Stick with saying "dress shirt" and you'll probably be okay.

Collars

Here's a list of the types of collars that differentiate the styles of dress shirts. I'm listing these in the order that most people consider less formal to most formal. You'll notice that I've also included suggestions about what type of collar looks best with certain face shapes:

Button-down: These shirts have collars that are buttoned to the shirtfront. These shirts can easily be worn without a tie.

Straight-point: The *V*-shaped points of a straight-point collar are the most common style, and are flattering for most faces.

Spread: As you might guess based on the name, this shirt's points are cut so that they face away from each other. This creates a wider gap in the middle. This is a dressier type of shirt, and because of the spreading effect, they look better on men with slimmer faces.

Tab: With a higher collar and a smaller spread, this is most flattering on men with long necks.

Club: Also known as a rounded collar, the club collar is short, has rounded tips, and looks very stylish, though it's less commonly seen.

Pinned: With a high collar much like the tab collar, a pinned collar has a straight pin that fastens the two points.

Collars that don't have buttons or pins will be held in place with either plastic or metal stays to keep them from curling. The stays are inserted through holes in the underside of the collar and keep the ends of the collar from curling up. Better-quality shirts will have these stays in them when you buy them, and you should look for shirts with this feature. Don't throw away the stays when you unwrap your new shirt, and make sure to remove them when you wash your dress shirt. Tab collars have a piece of fabric sewn on each side and are secured with snaps or another type of fastener.

Cuffs

Cuffs are the other feature that distinguishes the type or style of dress shirt. Most dress shirts have barrel cuffs—usually one, sometimes two, or even three buttons close the ends of the sleeves. Depending on if you have either very thin or very thick wrists and forearms, you may find one style or another more comfortable. The other type of cuff is called a French cuff. Instead of having buttons, these shirts have two slits stitched into them so that you can insert cuff links to hold them closed in place of buttons. Some guys swear by a French cuff, but while I like the looks of cuff links, I generally think that simpler is better. For everyday business wear, go with button cuffs, and for those special occasions when you are wearing a suit, you may want to have a French cuff shirt hanging around.

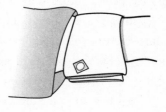

Sizing

Dress shirts are sold either in nominal sizes—small, medium, large, and extra large—or in numeric sizes corresponding to sleeve length and neck size. I don't recommend doing the measurement yourself; most good department and men's stores will have someone on hand who can measure you. The nominal sizes do have corresponding numeric sizes, but those vary somewhat from shirtmaker to shirtmaker. I always buy shirts based on the numeric sizing to ensure the proper fit. If you want to go the S/M/L/XL route, you really do need to try them on. As a rough guide, a large will fit a man with a 16–16½ inch neck and a 42–44 inch chest; medium a 15–15½ neck; and small a 14–14½ inch neck. This gets really tricky with sleeve length, which varies, so again, try those S/M/L/XL shirts on. One size does not even come close to fitting all.

Ironing a Dress Shirt

Some people don't like to wear 100 percent cotton shirts because of the wrinkle factor. Today, some 100 percent cotton shirts are treated with wrinkle reducers, so look for that feature. Whether your shirt is wrinkle-resistant or not, every guy should know how to iron a shirt. I know that many professionals take their shirts to a laundry or dry cleaner to get it done (it is still only laundered at the dry cleaner, not dry cleaned; a cotton shirt should not be subject to dry cleaning), but you can save yourself quite a few dollars a month if you do it yourself. Also, you never know when you're going to be on a business trip or when you might need a shirt right away and no laundry or dry cleaner can help you out.

Here's how to iron a dress shirt:

Step 1: Set up the ironing board. Fill the iron with water and plug in the cord.

Step 2: Dial the iron to the steam-heat setting appropriate for the fabric of the shirt. You'll find the fabric listed on the shirt label.

Step 3: With the shirt unbuttoned, flatten the collar and smooth it onto the ironing board. Iron the collar flat.

Step 4: Button the shirt and prepare to iron the sleeves. Hold the shirt with one hand at the shoulder of the sleeve. With the other hand, flatten the cuff at the natural crease. Smooth the sleeve straight, following the cuff crease, and lay it on the ironing board. Iron the cuff flat, and then iron the rest of the sleeve. Avoid forcing a shoulder crease. Repeat for the second sleeve.

Step 5: Slip the entire shirt around the narrow end of the ironing board with the collar at the pointed end. Rotate the shirt so that the buttons are on the surface of the board running parallel to the length of the board. Iron the front panel of the shirt, carefully moving the front point of the iron in between the buttons. Rotate the shirt to iron the entire front panel.

Step 6: Rotate the shirt until the first half of the back panel is flat on the surface of the ironing board. Iron the entire back panel, rotating the shirt as necessary. Take care to angle the shirt so that you can iron the top shoulder panel.

Step 7: Iron the shirt's remaining front panel. Rotate the shirt to bring forward the remaining front panel and iron it.

Step 8: Immediately hang the dress shirt on a hanger.

Step 9: Break down the ironing station: Turn off and unplug the iron, and pour out any remaining water. Coil the cord and store the iron in an open area, away from children, until it cools. Fold and store the ironing board.

Folding a Dress Shirt

Most of the time, you're going to want to hang your dress shirts. They will get fewer wrinkles that way. If you are traveling, you will also want to take a hanging bag so that your shirts and suits won't get creased. But sometimes it's not possible to hang your clothes while traveling and you have to fold them. I've been in clothing stores and marveled as clerks and cashiers have folded clothing so neatly and quickly. It wasn't until I was in the navy and had to fold *everything* neatly that I figured out how to handle tricky things like a dress shirt. Here's the method I use:

Step 1—Prepare the shirt for folding
Lay the shirt flat, making sure it's buttoned. Fully buttoning the shirt will ensure a tight, wrinkle-free fold.

Step 2—Fold the sleeves to the middle of the back of the shirt
Fold in each sleeve horizontally, so that the cuffs cross over the middle of the back. In other words, the cuffs will form a small *X*. Be sure that the shirt's side seams are *not* folded in.

Step 3—Fold the sides to the middle
Fold in both sleeves again, this time bringing the shirt's side seams in evenly from shoulder to hem, so they meet under the collar, forming a broad *V* shape there. (The sides won't necessarily meet farther down the shirt.)

Step 4—Fold in half lengthwise

Holding the bottom of the shirt with two hands, fold the shirt in half lengthwise from the bottom up, so that the bottom edge of the shirt rests below the bottom of the collar. (Do this once or twice, depending on the length of the shirt and how much storage space you have.)

Step Five—Prepare for storage

Flip folded shirt over and store.

Choosing the Right Color

Besides the style and care of your shirts, you will have to make some decisions about what color shirt to wear. I like to vary the color of the shirts I wear. Of course, I have the old standby never-out-of-fashion, never-looks-out-of-place white shirt, but I don't limit myself to one color. A light blue generally works well with most outfits, but you'll also want to experiment, too. The colors that work best for you will depend on your skin tone and the color of the other pieces of your outfit that day. For African American men, I've found a helpful Web site, www.splendicity.com/metrostylemen/.

Beyond Solids

Adding a patterned dress shirt to your wardrobe is another way of putting your own touch on your look. Stripes of all different widths go in and out of fashion, so you have to be somewhat careful about this multicolored option. Generally, your better department stores are only going to carry what is currently in vogue, while your discount and outlet stores will be a good place to pick up a top-quality shirt at a lower price. A word of caution: there's a reason those shirts are in a discount or outlet store. They are generally not top sellers or are at the tail end of a trend. Still, if you find something that works for you at the right price, grab it.

Besides stripes, there are some dress shirts that are known as tattersall—a pattern of colored lines forming squares on a solid background. As you've probably figured out, they are plaid, but a more subdued type. Generally, with nonsolid color shirts, it is best to go with something subtle—shirts that at a distance appear to be one color, but when examined more closely are patterned. One of the reasons why a patterned dress shirt can be a trickier option is that you have to find a tie pattern (unless you go with a solid color tie) that doesn't clash with the pattern in the shirt. There's a concept in the military when it comes to camouflage: you can either try to blend in—like the desert pattern soldiers wear while in Iraq—or you can dazzle and confuse people by using bright colors and patterns. A good concept in battle, but not in getting dressed.

Tie It Up

Before you can tie a tie, you have to buy a tie. Choosing a tie is sometimes one of the more difficult tasks men undertake. Here are a few "rules" you can follow to help you when you have a patterned shirt:

1. Choose a tie that repeats the dominant color in your shirt. If you have a cerulean blue shirt, find a tie with a stripe, polka dot, or abstract shape in it that matches that cerulean blue.

2. If you're going to wear a checked shirt and a checked tie, make sure the larger pattern is in the tie and the smaller pattern in your shirt.

3. Vary the weight of your patterns. In other words, if you have a shirt with thin stripes, wear a tie with thick stripes, and vice versa. Don't wear a shirt and a tie with similarly thick stripes or checks.

There are a multitude of Web sites you can consult to give you advice about ties and shirts, including www.necktieadvisor.com, www.lifeinitaly.com/fashion/fashion-men, and www.gq.com. The last of these is produced by the publishers of *GQ* and *Details* magazines.

Dressing for Success in Your Environment

As I mentioned, business has moved in a more casual direction over the years, and you'll want to match your level of dress to your work setting. The next step down from a suit is a jacket and tie. Still a pretty formal look that requires some effort, probably even more than a suit as far as mixing and matching. But a jacket and tie is appropriate for almost any business setting and you can ask a salesperson for help making sure ties and jackets match, as well as following the advice I offered earlier.

Trousers and dress shirt with nice shoes and a belt are acceptable for day-to-day work in many offices. Some consider this "business casual" and only okay on Fridays.

The online career site Monster.com offers some basic suggestions that make a great deal of sense. Among these are consistency, consideration, and courtesy. The first of these is especially true if your company has a business casual Fridays-only policy, but it also applies if that dress policy extends throughout the week. If you typically wear a suit to work and you show up one day in a pair of cargo shorts and a T-shirt, that's going to be very jarring to everyone. The same is true in a more casual environment. How you dress creates certain expectations about you, so don't vary too widely. If your business-casual approach is to wear a sport coat and a dress shirt with no tie, that's a very respectable look to establish yourself in a number of environments.

In terms of consideration, you need to consider what you're going to be doing on a particular day (meetings, lunch appointments, and so on) as well as what your fellow employees are wearing. As for courtesy, this may be the simplest way to avoid any potential conflicts: If your company doesn't have a written policy, then ask someone in human resources about what the parameters are. If you have a specific question, ask it before you wear that article of clothing.

A final *C* that I would add is this: conservative. It is better to err on the side of caution than it is to err on the side of inappropriateness. That means that sport coats and shirts or dress pants and casual or dress shirts (without a tie) are always safe options. Here are few more specific suggestions.

Pants

The default choice that many men opt for in a business-casual environment is to wear chinos—a coarse-weave cotton fabric. These come in a variety of colors and in plain front or pleated. For many men, chinos seem to be the only option, and khaki dominates the field of play. Chinos are fine, but if they are your only option, you'll probably grow tired of them. Many fashion experts suggest that you still opt for the tailored look of dress pants in a variety of fabrics. Wool dress pants, again either pleated or plain front, without a matching suit coat are always fashionable and comfortable. Even though blue, gray, and black are the common colors, it is okay to vary from that palette with pants, but save the red-and-green plaid pants for outside of work.

Shirts

Polo shirts come in a variety of colors and fabric weaves, and are great when matched with dress pants or more casual chinos. For variety and to add a more dressy look, oxford cloth dress shirts worn without a tie are good, too. Among the most popular current looks is one that really isn't so current: the gingham shirt. Gingham is a bold checked pattern that goes all the way back to the seventeenth century. As a choice for a business casual look with or without a jacket, it's a classic look that has now become trendy.

As a general rule, T-shirts are to be worn underneath another outer shirt. Slogan T-shirts, particularly with possibly offensive words or images on them, are always a no-no for work or other public places. The last thing you want to do is run into your boss at the mall on a weekend and have your shirt say something unflattering about *you*.

Shoes

For the most part, sneakers are not appropriate business casual attire—unless you're going to the company picnic. Look back at the chapter on footwear to see which are considered more casual. You won't go wrong with them. Whether you are wearing a suit, jacket and tie, or just slacks and a shirt, your shoes and belt should match: brown shoes with brown belt, black shoes with black belt. It's nice if you have more than one watch to make sure that your watchband matches as well, but it's not necessary. A stainless steel watch will go with everything if you want to buy one watch so you never have to think about it.

How you choose to dress is a conscious choice, and you are sending a message as a result. I believe in sending the most positive message possible about myself at all times. How you dress is a direct representation of how much you value yourself. Don't you want to let people know that you think you matter, that you are important, that you are someone worthy of respect? I don't want to leave you with the impression that it is important to always pay the most money to look your best and to value yourself most highly. Being neat and clean and taking good care of your shoes and clothes is what matters most. We'll talk about orderliness in other areas of your life in the next chapter.

CHAPTER SIX

COMMAND AND CONTROL: DEVELOPING A PLAN FOR YOUR LIFE

Returning to the metaphor of a book and its cover, we've spent some time discussing the cover to the book that is your life—that outward appearance that people will evaluate and judge you by when they first meet you. Are you clean and presentable with well-groomed hair? Are your clothes clean, stylish, and well pressed? Then your cover is good to go. Let's return now to the inside of the book that is you—the pages and chapters that make up your life. For a book to be good, it needs a good plot and a good character. These are the themes we'll explore in the next two chapters.

First, how aware are you of what the pages of your life or day-to-day routine look like? And do you know what might be happening in your life three chapters from now? Where are you headed? Second, in the following chapter, I take a look at the main character in the book that is your life: you. How do you establish an identity that satisfies you and will allow you to achieve all of your dreams? And if you find that you are not happy with who you are, how do you go about overhauling your character in a constructive way? I frequently speak in front of groups about my life experiences and the most common question afterward is how I not only made it out of the ghetto but actually found a successful career as a screenwriter. There are other questions, too. Why did I want to be a writer? When did my dream of becoming a writer first form in my mind? How did I "make it" in Hollywood? What do I most enjoy about writing? I've already answered some of those questions, but I am fully aware of how unlikely it is that I would be doing what I do today. In some sense, I'm a good candidate to be a writer. I've had varied and colorful experiences from which I can draw. I was always a keen observer, prone to introspection. And I have some talent as a visual artist that I can utilize as a writer.

On the other hand, I never had the kind of formal training or education that many writers have. To be self-educated in any field is to be called an autodidact. Many people without access to schools or formal education become autodidacts by teaching themselves through reading. Because I am dyslexic, reading is a time-consuming and laborious project for me and I'm not nearly as well-read as I'd like to be. If I were, let's say, a novelist instead of a screenwriter, that might be a problem. But I write screenplays—movies are my thing, and I love going to see them. I have been able to educate myself in the world of films by watching and learning. I mostly try to enjoy films when I watch them and leave my professional perspective at the door. It's such an incredible form of artistic expression and it's amazing how many different and great films are made every year.

Work

So why do I write? One of the real pleasures I find in writing is that I'm the one who is in control. My characters do what I tell them to do, say what I tell them to say, and quiet down and go away whenever I walk away from my computer. Of course, that's not how real life works at all. We're almost never in complete control in any situation. I've always been somewhat fascinated in my adult life by this idea of control and also of letting go of control. How could I find a way to enjoy both those experiences—being in complete command and surrendering control? Why is it that I don't mind driving fast in a car, but I feel uncomfortable when I'm a passenger in a fast-moving car? Why is it that I can entrust my life to someone I've not met to safely fly me and my family in a jet? Why is it that some people I know love roller coasters and others hate the sensation of not being able to stop, slow, or steer the car they are riding in?

Control has frequently been an issue in my life. When I was a kid growing up in the Picketts' house, I felt too often like my life was not my own. I would act out as a way to take control of the moment—even if the act was negative. All kids go through that, but when you don't have your parents in your life, when you're shuttled from one home to another, you feel more acutely the frustration of not having something at the center of your life holding things in place. Conversely, when you do have people in your life—in my case foster parents who might as well have been strangers—dictating your every move, you rebel against those constraints. While my personal circumstances growing up might have been a bit different and more challenging than yours, we all share that need to evolve from creatures who make limited choices about their lives to adults who are expected to make all the choices. And even when we are able to make every decision that affects us, there are always a thousand factors and events that will influence us.

Lately, in my work life, I've been writing a film adaptation of another work. Unlike a screenplay that is totally original, an adaptation takes a previously written or conceived work and translates it for the screen. Writing a screenplay from another source isn't something I frequently do, and I've been both frustrated and fascinated by the process. On the one hand, I didn't have to invent the main character's experiences; they were already there. But on the other hand, I am restricted by the fact that I have to follow what was already written. I can't invent details and incidents because my screenplay is based on a true story. I am both in control of writing the screenplay and controlled by the facts I was handed from which I cannot vary. Once when I hit a particularly frustrating moment, I decided to take a break and watch some television.

There was a breaking (and heartbreaking) story that morning about a man who had apparently killed his wife and five children in a murder-suicide. He had lost his job and could no longer pay the bills. According to a letter he sent to a Los Angeles news station, he decided along with his wife that it was better that they all die. Of course, the neighbors were shocked that this happened, and they said the usual kinds of things about not believing this could happen to what appeared to be a normal family living next door. As a husband and father, the story naturally upset me. What could possibly make anyone feel that this kind of dramatic step was the best way out of a situation? How desperate and how out of control must you feel in order to do something so horrible? And as awful as this event was, it seems as if there's one like it in the news every day. How many lives are in the process of spinning out of control out there, and how can we be sure ours is never one of them?

Later that same day, I was speaking with my manager about that same script and I mentioned the story I heard on the news. I commented on the idea of control and how I felt as if I was losing control of the material. As much as I like having control of my characters, when I'm really in the flow of my writing, the characters seem to come to life and exert their own demands on me. Confusing, right?

There was a pause on the other end of the line and then my manager said, "Control is an illusion, anyway."

I replied, "What are you talking about? We can control things. You drive your car down the road safely, you're in control."

"Sure, you think you are, but what if the guy who assembled the steering rod in your car's front suspension was having a bad day when your car was being built? What if his wife was upset with him because she thought he was spending too much money betting on football games and his team, which was up by four points with a minute to go, had fumbled the ball and the other team scored and he lost $400? What if he goes to work and he's distracted? He's thinking about those final moments of the game instead of his job and he doesn't torque down the bolt holding that assembly to the proper specifications. Years later you're driving and you have to swerve suddenly to avoid somebody who's distracted and drifting over into your lane. The linkage breaks and you end up going head-on into the other lane of traffic."

"That's a lot of what-ifs."

"So are you really in control of things or not?"

After we hung up, I thought more about what my manager had said, and I realized that if I thought about all the possible consequences and what-if scenarios that go into the simplest actions, I'd go crazy. Did I walk around all day just pretending that there was some order in the universe? Was he saying that the choices and the decisions that I make are determined by forces other than my own will? After I'd finally arrived at a point in my life where I felt like I was in control, was I just kidding myself? But when it came to my writing, wasn't I really the one who was clearly in charge? Of course I had to get input from other people about my work, but at the very least weren't my ideas entirely my own?

What Really Matters

Ultimately, I decided it didn't matter if control was an illusion or not. What mattered was that there were some things I could control and some things that I couldn't. I'd made it as far as I had because I'd taken control of my actions and decisions. The navy taught me a lot about personal responsibility, and because of that, I was able to reach my dream of writing thanks to hard work and a little bit of luck.

We all need to do things in our lives that gives us that sense of control, even when the universe around us seems ruled by chaos. We hear and read all kinds of stories every day about natural disasters or even an economy that swings up and down, taking good jobs with it when things go south. If we dwelled on those things for too long we'd become frozen by inaction. But if the economy is bad, you can't sit on your hands lamenting how you have no control over it—no one does! What you do have to do is get up off your butt and go looking for one of the good jobs that are out there.

The Practical Steps

Okay, so enough philosophizing. What I want to share with you is how I learned to hold off that chaos in a more practical way. Maybe being organized and having a place for everything and everything in its place can't answer all those questions about life, but it can make it easier and more manageable. Developing disciplined habits and routines, keeping your things organized, and performing personal maintenance work puts you in charge of your life to the fullest extent possible. Again, it would have been easy for me as a young person to play the victim, and sometimes I did feel that way. It was only after I acquired strategies to get my act together that I was able to take control of my life and get it moving in the direction I wanted it to go. Too many times, I hear young people (and not-so-young people) putting the blame on external circumstances for their failures and struggles. You've taken control of your appearance by grooming properly, dressing appropriately, and taking care of your wardrobe. Now it's time to tackle other aspects of your life and get them squared away. Once you take control of these things, you've built the foundation upon which success comes. Step one in taking command of your own life is getting yourself organized.

Developing a Routine

As you know, my life with the Picketts was all about discipline. For better or worse, it might very well have been the one constant in an otherwise totally unpredictable environment. There was a strict schedule that had to be followed even on weekends. Later on in the navy, the routine was much the same, except cleaning wasn't confined to Saturdays, as it was with the Picketts. Life in the navy is rigidly organized. If you were told to report for duty at 0600 hours, that meant 0600 hours. Meals were served during specific blocks of time and you had better get there before the mess decks shut down or you were out of luck. Period. In basic training those rules were applied even more strictly, and being in an unfamiliar environment and having lived a life of such great uncertainty previously, this regimen actually helped me feel secure in a way I never had before. Once I gained that security, it started to free up my intellect to pursue—and even enjoy—the ways of the world.

So much of life is about finding balance, and that's true with developing a personal routine. Most of us are more habituated than we might imagine, and a lot of times you'll hear friends complain that their lives are boring because there isn't a lot of variation from one day to the next. If you've ever seen the movie *Groundhog Day* (and I recommend that you do), then you saw Bill Murray take this everyday-is-the-same to hilarious extremes. If you start to let yourself feel like you are in a rut when you are young, I promise you the feeling will only get worse as the years go by. I'll touch on this again shortly, but structuring my day and my life was one of the great positive steps I took, so I recommend it to you without hesitation.

Routine Emergencies

One of the advantages of having a routine and being trained the way we were in the navy was that it gave us something we could fall back on in case of an emergency. We were well prepared because we trained all the time and ready for every contingency. In January of 2009, a US Airways flight leaving New York's LaGuardia airport struck several geese, immediately disabling both engines. Unable to return to the airport, the pilot had to look for a safe place to land his aircraft with 155 souls aboard. Incredibly, he chose the Hudson River. Chesley "Sully" Sullenberger and his crew safely brought the plane down in the river, and miraculously no one was seriously injured. The flight attendants and crew were even able to get everyone off the plane in an orderly fashion. Passengers reported that most folks remained calm and everyone followed the emergency instructions. The reason why this "miracle on the Hudson" ended so well was because of the training and preparation the crew members had. They'd practiced those procedures so often that they were able to remain calm, to go into a kind of autopilot, and do their jobs well.

That's what order and routine can do for you. At times of great stress, having something you can rely on and fall back on—even if it just means getting dressed and going to work—can help you focus on the other matters at hand. It might sound like a small thing, but your routine can be the constant that lets you get through the hard times and maximize the good ones. We probably won't be called up for something nearly as dramatic as what Sully accomplished, but we are all the pilots of our own lives and careers, and we have a responsibility to the people around us.

My Routine

I know that I have certain routines when it comes to my writing. In terms of scheduling, I see the kids off to school, take a walk with LaNette, then go to my office. I do most of my writing in the morning, reserving the lunch and afternoon hours for meetings. By the time the kids come home from school, I like to be done with my work. That doesn't always happen, but I control what I can and let go of the rest.

I also have a routine when it comes to my desk. I have an assigned place for everything. To limit distractions, I only have the project I'm working on in front of me. I use an hourglass to remind me to stand and stretch every hour as a break. I also keep a bottle of water to my right and the telephone to my left. I wear a headset for the telephone so that I can keep writing even when I have to take a call. I alternate between using a hard-wired keyboard for sitting and writing and a wireless keyboard for writing while standing. I have to wear comfortable clothes (when writing at home that usually means I'm writing in pajamas—so much for my uniform). I keep the room really dark when I begin a project and play music that inspires me. As I make progress and I gain more control, I begin letting light into the room by opening the blinds.

I'm not obsessive; I just like things to be a certain way. I won't freak out if something happens that affects my regimen. As a writer, I am self-reliant in a way that I might not be in another profession. In an office, for example, a boss might pop his head in to see how you're doing on that project due Tuesday. You could be assigned something along with a colleague who might monitor your work alongside you. At the very least, people will notice whether you show up or not! But I am boss, employee, and colleague all rolled into one. Anyone who is launching his own business will find himself in a similar situation until he takes on more employees. But the reality is that we all also have stretches of time in our lives during which we are solely in charge. A teacher might have assigned you an essay due three weeks from today. Are you going to start your research today? Tomorrow? A week from tomorrow? Are you going to wait until the last day and try to pull an all-nighter? Only you can make those decisions for yourself. You determine what your routine is for getting schoolwork done. In turn, that routine will help establish whether you excel as a student or whether you struggle.

Making Things Easier

A few months ago, I came across a piece of software that's available for Apple computers. It's called Bento. I was intrigued from the beginning because the name invoked the love of Japan I developed in the navy. I have fond memories of eating bento box lunches in Japan. *O-bento* is what the Japanese call a packed meal, usually lunch. If you haven't already ordered one in a Japanese restaurant, bento boxes have internal dividers, and sometimes several stacked layers, so different kinds of food sit in their own little compartments. The whole thing is usually wrapped together with chopsticks in a cloth or special bag, and the goal is to make the package as attractive as possible, from the color combinations of the food to the presentation of the box and everything that accompanies it. Like much about Japanese culture, there's an aesthetic and utilitarian value to these boxes.

The Bento software does a similar kind of thing. It coordinates data from several different programs—e-mail, address book, calendar, etc.—to help me stay better organized. I needed something like that because as much as I try to do that myself, I sometimes find it takes me more time than I really want to spend. If I consider myself valuable, then my time is just as valuable, as well. An important part of bringing structure to our lives and taking control is making sure we are on top of our game. If a leading company like Apple is willing to sell me a program that helps me run my life "ship shape," well then, I am going to take full advantage. It doesn't have to be all that fancy, either. Chances are even the cell phone in your pocket has some kind of calendar function that can help you remember important dates and arrival times in the coming weeks. And you can use these tools to make sure you are spending the right amounts of time on the important aspects of your life—family, work and/or school, friends, charitable work, and so on. How do you know how you are spending your time?

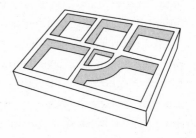

Many young people don't develop the routines and establish the schedules needed to be successful. One of the key things a schedule does is straighten out priorities. If you have even the loosest of schedules, you can identify what is important to you. If you haven't really been keeping track of what you do in a given day, here's an idea for how to get started. During the course of the day, in a spiral notebook, keep track of what you are doing at one-hour, half hour, and even fifteen-minute intervals. This is your unscheduled schedule. At the end of the day, before turning in, look at your list and tally the number of hours you spent involved in similar activities: eating, sleeping, reading, working, watching TV, playing a sport, talking on the phone or texting with friends, surfing the Internet, listening to music. What tops the list? Look for trends in how you spend your time.

The next step is to look at your schedule as it now exists and identify what the problem spots are for you—the activities that are wasting your valuable time and keeping you from accomplishing important goals. Let's say you're struggling with your grades.

Compare how much time you spend studying with how much time you spend hanging out with friends. It may be that you are spending a lot of your time working, and your grades may be suffering because of that. Are you putting in so many hours at work because you have to meet tuition and other expenses? Or do you like the few luxuries that some extra money brings? There are only so many hours in a day, and you'll have to negotiate some give-and-take in order to spend the most time at your highest priority activities.

Too many people feel that their lives are out of control and that their fate isn't in their own hands. For the most part, that's not true. By knowing how you use your time, and using your time wisely, you can give yourself the best opportunity to succeed, and also to have more fun, knowing that you are in charge and you can play as well as work, just in the right amounts. These are skills that will serve you your whole life.

Routine or Rut?

Just because you have a routine in place doesn't mean that you can never break out of it. Whether that means taking a different route to work (or even walking or riding a bike instead of driving or taking public transportation), varying what you eat for breakfast so that it's not the same bowl of cereal every day, even sitting at a different lunch table with a different group of people, a break in your routine can help you see things from a different perspective. Once you have established a schedule that works, even if you never vary from it, you run the risk over time of falling into ruts. Predictable is good, especially for someone like myself who never had that security, but there is a flip side to security if it limits new experiences or discoveries. Striking a balance between the routine and the unexpected is important. As much as I felt like the navy had saved me and given my life structure and meaning, by the end of my time there I again wanted more freedom and more of a chance to make different decisions about my own valuable time.

Ironically, I became a prison guard and spent many hours in one of the most strictly controlled environments imaginable. Everything we did was dictated by the clock. It was important for prisoners to adapt to that rigid lifestyle, but as a guard I could observe its effects. One day, an inmate told me that he'd purposely committed another crime after being released from prison because he wanted to get caught. He couldn't deal with life outside of prison and all its uncertainties and choices. I felt bad for him, and our conversation made me realize how important that balance between control and lack of control needs to be. It's important that young people develop a schedule for themselves—not one that's dictated by others. Waking up each morning and going to school or work at the same time, going to the gym to work out a few times a week (more on this later), having regularly scheduled social time with friends and/or family all help keep you on a path toward achieving your goals. But it all starts with you.

The Bigger Picture

Daily routines and schedules are the road on which your life travels. You want that road to be as smooth and well maintained as possible. But that still raises the question, where exactly is that road headed? That's where goals enter the picture as important destination points in life's journey. I've mentioned several times the importance of setting goals, which is not something that I've always consciously done myself. It's hard to establish goals when you're young, and looking back, I don't think many of my friends had them when we were growing up together in Cleveland. As hard as it is to establish control when you feel like there is no security, it's even harder at those moments to be able to think ahead to what you really want to accomplish. I almost literally stumbled into the military because I needed to survive—I needed to be fed and housed and protected. But those kinds of desperate decisions are not the best and they don't always have the same happy results mine did.

Even after the navy, until I knew that I wanted to write and share my life story in a book and a movie, I was pretty much just drifting. Don't expect goals to be readily apparent, and don't become frustrated if it takes you awhile to identify your goals and then the way to achieve them. You will.

The Goal is . . . Having a Goal

I learned some lessons as I found my way in the world that I hope you can apply to your own life. Even though I didn't have something like a formal five-year plan, even if I didn't know precisely what my destination was, I did have a vision of what I wanted my life to be like. I'm really fortunate that I got there. But perhaps if I had applied some of the things I'd learned when I was younger, I might have arrived at this happy place much sooner. And one of those things that I learned, especially as my career as a writer developed, was to set intermediate goals for myself. These are smaller steps on the path to successfully completing a project. As I mentioned earlier, as a self-employed individual, it's all on me to get it done. If I have to write a screenplay that is due in six months, when do I want the outline completed? When should I finish the first draft to allow me at least one other draft before the deadline arrives? If you have a report for work that is due in two weeks, when will you have your initial research done? When will you put together a draft of your PowerPoint presentation? On a bigger scale, if you want to find a job by November, when will you complete your résumé? When will you have bought an appropriate outfit for interviews? You get the idea. Sometimes a long-term goal seems imposing or out of reach and what you need is short-term deadlines to motivate yourself.

Breaking down long-term tasks with short-term goals is helpful when it comes to crafting the screenplay of your life. You should have some final goal for yourself—career, family, contribution to society. But you need to break that goal down into manageable steps. What can you do that day, that week, that month, that year, to get you closer to your goal? That's one of the reasons why I asked you to keep track of how you spend your time. If you look at what you did on a given day and you see that none of it has anything to do with your long-term goals, then you need to either reevaluate your goal or how you plan to get there.

Be Prepared to Alter Your Plan

I spend much of my time as a writer on the process of rewriting. The first draft is always the fun part. Your ideas are fresh and new, the task is just beginning. I am always excited at this point. Revising your initial draft isn't nearly as much fun, especially if you do it because a studio's feedback indicates that what you thought was so great isn't something they are too keen on. Just as you need flexibility in developing routines and schedules, you need to have flexibility with your goals and the timeline you've set for yourself. Once I set the goal, it took many more years to see *Antwone Fisher* arrive in theaters than I would have ever imagined. I had to write many drafts (forty-two of them) before Twentieth Century Fox acquired the rights to my life story. That's a lot of rewriting and reenvisioning, but with each successive script I've worked on, that number has decreased. I've learned things along the way.

You can't expect instant success or be frustrated each time the path you've imagined for yourself takes some unanticipated turn. That's where flexibility comes into play. If you plan for those detours, even if you don't know when or where you will encounter them, you'll weather setbacks better and bounce back faster. I know now that when I turn in a draft of a screenplay to a studio executive, I'm not going to get immediate approval—hardly anyone does. I'm going to have to do more work. That's okay. I know that we're all trying to make the best product possible.

That's the same attitude you'll need for the inevitable changes you will have to make in your life's plan. Not everything will go exactly as hoped for, but that's okay. Remember those scenes in movies where the frustrated writer crumples up a page and tosses it in the garbage? That's not quite how it works in real life. Success isn't always about starting from scratch. Whether it's a screenplay, a report for work, or a homework assignment, learning from mistakes, taking criticism in a constructive way and showing you can learn from it, and then making improvements on your work are all critical skills. If a teacher offers you criticism for a homework assignment, what can you learn from it so that next time you don't make the same mistake? If teachers see you taking their words seriously, they will spend more time trying to help you improve in class.

Back It Up

One of the things the navy taught us when we were stationed overseas was that we had to be careful leaving and returning to our base. For safety reasons, we didn't want to get into the habit of following the same route every time. They asked that we develop alternate routes—at least three different ones. Even though the navy tried to impress on us the idea of being prepared, I didn't always take it to heart. I remember several times in my rush to get off base to go to a nightclub or out with friends, I'd forget to fill up the tank before I took off. Sure enough, I'd find myself in a bad neighborhood at night, refueling. These are the kinds of situations that can escalate into unnecessary emergencies if we don't take the time to think through our plans.

For example, maybe your dream is to become a professional athlete or entertainer. Who can blame you? Fame and fortune await those who succeed in those fields. The trouble arises when you put all your eggs in the basket of skyrocketing to athletic success or going gold with your first single. For every superstar such as Kobe Bryant, Tom Brady, or will.i.am, and for every Will Smith or Brad Pitt, thousands and thousands of aspiring actors, recording artists, and athletes either labor in anonymity or don't work in their desired profession at all. While I encourage everyone to pursue their dreams, it is also important to have a plan in mind and to have a back up plan to support that big dream. While focusing 100 percent of your efforts on a big dream can lead to success, you need to balance that with an alternative option. There is only so much that you can control in life. Some people are fortunate to receive the so-called break that launches a career. At the same time, most often when you hear that someone is an "overnight sensation," the reality is that they were working for their break for years or even decades. Very few stars were standing on line at the ice cream shop or playing baseball in the sandlot when they were discovered. Their hard work and dedication allowed them to capitalize on an opportunity when it came their way.

Balancing that belief in yourself and the reality that you might not have what it takes is difficult. No magic formula exists to help you determine whether you measure up or when it is time to hang it up and look in a different direction. Establishing goals is one way to set some guidelines for yourself as you pursue a long term plan. Perhaps if you don't get that big break, or even a little break, in five or ten years, it's time to follow a different path, one that will give you the support you need through life's ups and downs.

Does that mean that you abandon your original dream completely? Of course not. You modify it. You revise it. Maybe your love of the game, of singing, of acting, can be repurposed and lead to a related field—as a coach, as an audio engineer, as a camera operator. Better to work in a field directly related to something you love than to be one of those people working at a job they hate. Finding satisfaction in the work you do is one way to add to your value and to take control of your life.

All of my experiences, from being in foster care, to being homeless, to joining the navy, to working as a prison guard, then as a security guard at a movie studio, contributed in ways large and small, ways that I might not even recognize, to where I ended up. All the false starts and dead ends you may encounter when you set about shaping your life are important and do contribute to your ultimate success. When you view every experience you have as bringing you closer to your ultimate goal, you can squelch the feeling that your life is subject to forces beyond your control. While you may not be able to control everything that happens to you, you can control how you respond to events, you can control the general direction your life takes, and the more you control those thoughts, the greater the chances are that you will get where you want to go.

Think of it this way: You are the person writing the screenplay of your life story. You're going to get all kinds of notes—or feedback—from people about how the story should or could go. Take these notes seriously and learn to accept criticism as well as praise graciously. You have to develop the skill of filtering the good advice from the bad, and you'll learn who is trying to build you up and who is trying to tear you down. Ultimately though, the choice of which characters to include and exclude, what plot points are essential, what actions the hero of your story—you—takes, is in your hands. If life is a screenplay, why not be have a happy ending? We'll dwell a little more on this concept that you are the hero of your life's story in the next chapter.

CHAPTER SEVEN

INVENTING AND REINVENTING YOURSELF

In the last few weeks, my daughters, my wife, and I have started to play the board game Monopoly. We're not trying to teach our girls to flip real estate or prepare for more economic hard times to come. It's just a great family game and sure, we're all a little competitive with our little houses and hotels.

I've noticed that Azure, my youngest daughter, will roll the dice and then count out the number of spaces in her head. If she realizes she's landing on, say, Atlantic Avenue with three houses, depending on whether she owns it or not, she'll look at us with her beautiful eyes and smile happily, or put on her cutest expression and plead for an opportunity to roll the dice again before moving her piece. Of course, we tell her that she has to stick with her original roll, that what's fair is fair and there are rules that you must follow. When the kids were younger and we played games like Chutes and Ladders or the card game Uno, we sometimes let them have another go if they made a mistake or did not see the best move possible. We wanted to let them experience some of the joy of winning and succeeding more than we wanted them to learn that the world operates by rigid principles, and that once you made a move in a certain direction your fate was cast in stone and that was that.

The Do-Over

I remember my own days playing with kids in the neighborhood. I loved the do-over when I could wrangle one. I always felt that there was something magical in getting a second chance. Certain teachers too would extend that opportunity in an effort to get me to try, try again as I sometimes struggled. When one of my girls lands on Chance and goes directly to jail without passing Go and without collecting $200, my heart sometimes skips a beat when I think about extending a second chance, a do-over that will make everything all right. In golf, it is called a mulligan and sometimes in a casual game your buddies will let you take one after  you hooked a ball into the course's largest water hazard. But since we can't always take a mulligan when we make mistakes or draw a bad card, we must also learn to absorb the hit and move on. Of course, the one thing you can never do is cheat.

Pattern Recognition

When I look back over my life, I feel like there's a similarity between the two significant do-overs I've taken. In both instances, I made the choice, but the second time, I was in far greater control of my life. When we're kids, we have to enlist others to go along with our do-over; when we're older, we only have to ask ourselves for permission to try something new, to make an important change in our lives. And it doesn't always have to be a change motivated by a desire to make up for something that's lacking in our lives. Sometimes changing for the sake of changing, experimenting, and imitating can be an important step toward improving ourselves in ways that we initially didn't know we needed to or even wanted to.

When the moment came for me to enlist in the navy, I knew that I had few choices. My last social worker was named Bill Ward and he told me that a life in the military was just what I needed to get my life on track. I'd resisted the idea, still clinging to the thought I would go to art school. Through much of my childhood, my dream had been to be a professional artist, and even though I no longer said aloud that I was going to be the next Michelangelo, I felt like that early pencil sketch self-portrait was waiting to be colored in. But after a long cold night in a Cleveland alley, seeing a recruiting poster that promised fun and adventure, and having no other prospects for a job or a place to live, I was convinced that art school could wait, it was time to join the navy and see the world. Joining the navy was a cosmic chance to pick up the dice again and take a new roll. Had I not taken this do-over, I don't know that I could tell you I'd still be around.

Boys to Men

As we grow up, we seek an identity that feels right. Adolescence and young adulthood are all about figuring out who you are and who you want to be. When I chose to join the navy, as lucky as I was with the new direction my life took, I had to accept at that moment an option less than my dream of becoming an artist. But ultimately it was just a step along the way. I don't consider myself a Michelangelo and I'm okay with that. I've become someone other than a great master artist, but in ways that I don't think I could have ever imagined back then. I'm master of who I am and I've created a good life for myself and my family. Those years when I dreamed of becoming an artist were important. At a time when I desperately needed it, calling myself the next Michelangelo was an identity in which I could cloak and protect myself.

As boys, and even as men, we all want to think of ourselves as the hero of our story. As I moved away from my earlier dream, the navy fueled that feeling I had within myself that I could act that role. That recruiting campaign was effective because it offered adventure and action and challenges. What man doesn't want these exciting things? What man doesn't dream of traveling to far away places and facing crucial tests of courage and guile? I sometimes think that my exodus from the Picketts' home and my journey through the streets of Cleveland as a homeless boy meet all the criteria of a hero's journey. In some ways, I might have taken those steps because I needed that kind of quest to lead me out of the abuse of my childhood and into a manhood where I could start anew. It doesn't matter that I spent much of that time quite frightened; I still was out there in the world and trying the best I could to survive.

The Hollywood Spin on Heroism

There's no doubt that my thoughts about the journey we take as men have been shaped by my experience in Hollywood, as unusual as that may sound. After surviving the streets of Cleveland, traveling the world in the navy, it took Hollywood to help explain the hero's journey we all seek to undertake? *C'mon, Antwone*, you must be thinking. Well, let me share with you a little bit of what I learned from my time in Hollywood. It all starts with the movies themselves and how they are written. While an entire generation has passed since young men sat in movie theaters and watched the *Star Wars* saga unfold, the hero's journey has always been a part of Hollywood and movie making. Today, you can enroll in a screenwriting course and learn the basic steps of that journey, how it is reflected in myths from around the world, and how to use that template to shape a screenplay. When I was working on the Sony lot and later my screenplay for *Antwone Fisher*, I even heard that certain studios had memos that explained exactly what elements writers should use to capture the magic of this journey. This thinking went into stories like *The Lion King*, where a young cub must overcome the death of his father, the king, and return from exile to reclaim the crown.

If you've ever had to plead with a girlfriend to see a certain movie or had her change the channel while you were watching one of your favorites on a Sunday afternoon, then you know that many women just don't get some of the movies that appeal to us guys. These are films like *The Shawshank Redemption* or *Top Gun* and the previously mentioned *Star Wars*. These stories reinforce the hero's journey and allow us to reexperience some of the universal themes about our journey into manhood. Frequently, coming to terms with a father figure is an important element of the plot or of the character's back story. Think about *An Officer and a Gentleman*, if you've seen it. In some ways, I could identify with Richard Gere's Mayo, a sullen, angry young man who lost his mother when she committed suicide. His father is an ineffective, womanizing career navy man who was a bad father and role model. When Mayo bumps up against the drill sergeant played by Louis Gossett, Jr., without realizing it he encounters the kind of father figure he needs. In the last scene, Gere's character goes into the factory where his girlfriend works and literally sweeps her off her feet. It's a classic romantic hero move and one that many men might think of as corny, but deep inside have dreams of doing themselves. Just as important, by graduating from officer candidate school, by putting up with Sergeant Foley's harsh treatment, and by finally letting someone in and sharing the truth about how much he was hurting, Mayo earned the acceptance of an important male figure and the love of a beautiful woman. Pretty basic but powerful stuff. As you can see, movies are not only my artistic outlet, but a way for me to understand the world, as well, through the work of others. Films, books, even graphic novels or television shows, when they are intelligently made, are all great ways to learn more about the world and yourself.

There are a number of different ideas about what exactly that hero's journey entails, but from what I've read, most agree that one of the steps is the call to adventure. Without realizing it, I was falling into the pattern, and perhaps you are drawn to some of these same elements. There can be a universality to what we experience as boys becoming men. Once I was introduced to these concepts through film, I better understood the path I followed. Joining the navy during peacetime, I knew the chances of seeing combat were small, and to be honest, I wasn't really looking forward to being involved in it. I was more drawn to the notion of traveling to faraway places. I'd already withdrawn from my family (another of the steps) in preparation for setting out into the world. My homelessness was like the descent into the underworld, and the characters I met, in particular a street thug named Butch and my apprenticeship to him for a time, were all a part of this larger journey. Butch was a truly bad guy who held me in his sway at my darkest hour. But I suffered for this momentary weakness when he beat me up and I realized what a terrible character he was.

All of us will try on a number of identities in the course of our young lives. We all want to find a way to be the hero in the story, not the villain. That means something different for every one of us. The important thing is what lies at the heart of your character: values like integrity, honesty, virtue. What kind of music you listen to, how you comb your hair, or which political party you might favor are secondary to who you are. Spend some time and think about what lies at your core. Are you happy with it or are there ways you'd like to change? Remember, you write the script, so start today.

My Evolutionary Roles

I talked earlier about how my first identity was that of a victim. I'm not proud to say it, but it's true. Maybe I had a good reason to feel that way; I was born with a couple of strikes against me. I might not have known back then that my mother was an unwed teenager and my father died violently when he was a young man even before I was born, but I did know that I didn't have a family. Being without one made me a boy without a true identity, and that's a pretty tough deficit to start out with. For a long time my identity was shaped by the Picketts and their beliefs. As I touched on earlier, most of what they impressed on me was negative—that was the lens through which they saw and interacted with the world. Fear was a dominant presence in their household, and you can imagine that an identity based on fear is no identity at all.

I don't know what it was or where it came from, but I had the idea that life wasn't supposed to be the way Reverend Pickett preached. Deep down I knew that in this earthly life you could and should find some sort of enjoyment and pleasure. If the Picketts thought that life was tough and painful, they sure made it that way for me. The only way to break free from that pain was to find an identity based on the possible and the beautiful, thus the artist was born.

The first act in the birth of Antwone as the hero on his journey occurred one day when I refused to go to church. I'll tell you a little bit more about my religious experience later, but I'm sorry to say that the Picketts gave me a very poor perception of that institution when I was a child. Because I was so poorly treated and because Mr. Pickett carried the title of Reverand, I associated his character with the church's. To this day I can't tell you what wellspring of courage and resilience I drew from to state that I wasn't going to tread those church steps anymore. I had no real hope of gaining from my defiance and I had seen what happened to others in my house who dared to transgress. Maybe it was the sheer audacity of the enterprise that caught the Picketts off guard and allowed me to escape unharmed and victorious. I was fully prepared for the wrath of God and the wrath of the Picketts to come down on me. Neither happened. A couple of other things did occur, though. First, I realized that there was a part of me that would only put up with so much before I said, "That's it. I've had enough." The second was that, realizing I could take some control, I grew bolder. In the romanticized journey to manhood you see on the screen, there is always a scene during which a character finally makes a stand. A crucial part of putting together our identity is knowing what our limits are—establishing a boundary past which we aren't going to let anyone push us. It tells you how bad things were for me that this point was made about church. And I'm certainly not suggesting that you make the same point, no matter how much of your Sunday church takes away from touch football or morning TV.

While the cause I fought for was me, and that makes my action self-serving if not selfish, it was okay. I came to a crucial realization—some good could come of not always doing exactly as I was told. I felt a lot better about myself for having taken a stand, and better that it happened sooner rather than later. I didn't immediately triumph, but I don't think that I would be where I am today if I had not shed that victim identity. Over time, I'd overcome more and more of my reluctance to speak up and to act. Remember, the identity with which you started, or even the one you have as you hold this book in your hands, does not have to be the identity you have years from now if making that change is going to positively influence your life. I started as a victim because I was victimized. But I took hold of a spark within myself and it helped me to create a new identity.

Another Identity

When it came to time spent with girls, my identity was that of the "nice guy." At least nice guy was one step up from the wallflower I started out as. Because girls found me nonthreatening, they assigned me the role as much as I took it on. I came to think of myself around girls as the messenger boy and security guard. Girls trusted me with their secrets about who they liked, or they asked me to serve as their go-between and deliver messages to those boys. Even though I hoped that they would show a similar romantic interest in me, I at least had a chance to talk with them. I was the guy who would be asked to escort a girl home, but that was it. These were valuable lessons for me, and in my mind, I still saw something more for myself. But I treated girls with respect and I saw that they were individuals just like me. However you identify yourself, the hero acts appropriately and respects boundaries in his social life. I'm glad that whatever mistakes I did make growing up, being unkind to girls was not one of them.

Imagine

Inventing and reinventing your identity as you grow and change is a powerful act of the imagination. I was blessed with a powerful imagination and maybe that was the kernel that allowed me to break free. I'm not sure how my imagination developed, but it did. I used to rehearse scenarios in my head and then put them into practice in conversations. I would envision a certain encounter—one I wanted to have or one I didn't—and mentally play the scene out, rehearsing the lines I might say. I also pretended a lot. If I felt that someone didn't like me, I would imagine a scene in which I won them over with my wit or performed some heroic deed that helped them change their mind about me. Some of my more elaborate fantasies revolved around my family—the one I didn't know—and how great it was that they were out there looking for me. They were enduring their own trials and tribulations, but they endured them all because they wanted so much to rescue me from a horrible situation. Other times, I would engage my brain to create vivid scenarios that catapulted me from my surroundings into a better life. I don't recall all the specifics, but I used that tactic throughout my life, and it's something I still do today as a writer when I envision scenes and characters purely of my own creation. I'd imagine the nice apartment, furnishings, electronics, the elaborate parties I'd throw, the things I'd be able to do for friends. That allowed me to get excited about my prospects and it motivated me to improve my position in life. Without someone else to act as my cheerleader, I had to do that for myself in lots of different ways. Those fantasies of the good life were a necessary step. Had I not dreamed of my family, I might never have set out to find them as I ultimately did. Without that vision of who you want to be or what you want your life to look like, you won't ever advance beyond where you are.

Developing that vision of who you want to be and what you want your life to look like is the first step in inventing and reinventing yourself. It requires imagination, but also the ability to observe. I drew from a wide variety of sources—my friends, people in the neighborhood, people I worked with, people I'd seen on TV or at the movies, people whose music I admired—to come up with a concept of who and what I wanted to be next. For example, when I started in the navy, I started at the lowest rank possible. I quickly realized that there were others with a higher rank who had more privileges. Other sailors looked up to them. So from day one I did everything I could to advance and ultimately reach the rate of Third. I was determined to rise as high as I could as an enlisted guy.

In order to move up in rank, I had to take a servicewide test—in other words, I wasn't just competing against the serviceman E-5 on my ship hoping to move up to petty officer first class, but against every serviceman E-5 in the entire navy who took the test to advance in rate from Third to Second and ultimately to petty officer first class. Although I passed the test every time, I did not advance because of all the hundreds of people hoping to move up in rate, there were usually only ten or so slots in the higher rate available. So the highest rate that I achieved before being discharged was E-5, petty officer second class, which isn't bad. I never did get to first class, but that was okay with me. I also didn't reach my ultimate goal of becoming a chief petty officer.

After getting out of the navy, I continued to do whatever I could to support the U.S. Navy whenever called upon by participating in public service announcements to increase participation in the navy reserves. I also spoke at admirals' conferences, navy training events around the country, and I was the keynote speaker for the navy and other branches of the military. I tried to stay active and to give back to the navy because I felt the navy had done so much for me. I wanted to be a positive role model for young sailors.

Twenty years after I was discharged, on October 5, 2009, in a surprise ceremony held during a navy recruiting training event where I was the keynote speaker, I received an appointment to honorary chief petty officer from Force Master Chief Christopher L. Penton, master chief of Navy Recruiting Command USN. It is a great honor and a tremendous thrill to have had Master Chief Penton pin the Chief's Anchors on my lapels. I was also thrilled to be welcomed in by a multitude of U.S. navy chiefs, senior chiefs, and master chiefs who all stood in line to shake my hand. The point of this story is that if you believe in something, if it's good and true, you can continue to advance and achieve. It doesn't have to be over. It may take more time than you hope, but that vision can be realized. You just need to take the right steps.

Do It Before You've Done It

To make my dream more real, to make myself believe that I already had what it took to be a Petty Officer Third Class, I went and bought the stripes that I would wear on my uniform when I earned the rate. I put them in my locker as a reminder. I never gave up and took the test more than a few times before being promoted, but in my mind, I'd been rehearsing my position as a petty officer for a long time. By spending time with the second class petty officer I knew and being introduced to others in his circle, I gained invaluable experience and insight. I saw how officers conducted themselves and what their lives were like. Seeing concrete evidence of the benefits I'd get through a promotion motivated me further. When it was finally made official, the transition was relatively easy for me and the sense of satisfaction at having reinvented myself was tremendous. I'd put it out there that I expected more of myself and for myself, and I made it happen.

To summarize, the steps that you need to take to develop an identity or to reinvent yourself are the following:

- Develop your vision: decide who it is you want to be and what you want your life to look like.
- Find positive role models and examples: find people in your life or others you don't know who you admire and want to emulate.
- Use the power of words to your advantage: state your intentions to other people.
- Associate with a group of like-minded people: there is strength in numbers and much to learn from those who are at the level you want to attain.
- Find a powerful symbol to motivate you: find some symbol that you can use to serve as motivation and reward.

- Persevere: you can build your account through "sweat equity" and working hard.

Let's explore some of these points.

Find Positive Role Models

One of the great things about the navy was that it exposed me to people from all over the world. I traveled far and wide and that was exciting and educational. But I also met and learned from the wide variety of Americans with whom I served—sometimes in positive ways and sometimes in negative ones. These experiences worked together to expand my vision of the possibilities available to me. Growing up in Cleveland, living in foster care, going to a special placement school, and being homeless had given me tunnel vision. It was as if someone had put blinders on me and all I could see was the narrow world in front of me. And what I saw most frequently was people who either had given up on their dreams entirely or who had no power to think beyond their circumstances. The few dreamers I did know had no goal of ever making those dreams come true.

While it's ideal to have role models in your life to emulate, you might need to look beyond the next block over or even the same town if the right person isn't in your current environment. For example, I admired and wanted to be like Marvin Gaye. The soul of his music and its powerful social commentary made a deep impression on me. If you are not familiar with his album *What's Going On?*, you should be—it's one of the great works of R&B. Later on, I watched and listened and tried to learn from people outside my own circle of enlisted men and, after the navy, prison guards. As a lesson, I noted what the dreamers I knew said, but I wanted to be a reality maker. I paid attention to how pure dreamers never seemed to develop a plan and reflected on their inactivity to inspire my own efforts.

Once you are in the workplace, these role models are called mentors, and it's definitely an ingredient of success to find a mentor within your company or place of work. Having a mentor is a more engaging relationship than having a role model whom you admire from afar. A mentor can be anyone who has more experience than you and can help guide you, solve problems, open doors, and generally be a friendly ear when you need one. Bosses can definitely be mentors, and as you move up and on in the world, it's always a good idea to maintain a good relationship with former bosses who can continue to guide you in your industry. The flip side of role models and mentors is being the kind of person a mentor might want to take under his or her wing—to show the ambition and dedication at work or school. Many people higher up the chain enjoy helping up-and-comers, so it is not an imposition to create this kind of relationship. Just be sure your gratitude is clear, and don't overburden your mentor at a time when they might be under their own work pressure.

Use the Power of Words to Your Advantage

Putting the power of words to work for you can take a lot of different forms. After Todd Black hired me to write the script of *Antwone Fisher*, I began telling people that I was a writer. At first it felt a little uncomfortable since I hadn't actually published anything. People would ask me, "What have you written that I might have seen or read?" And I'd have to answer, "Nothing yet." The "yet" was important to me, but it was met with rolled eyes and more than one skeptical smirk. Since then, I've learned that many people will say or do something to put you in your place. Perhaps it's human nature, but too many people would rather see others fail than succeed. Maybe it's something that's meant to make them feel better about themselves, but the net result for anyone is zero. What you have to realize in these situations is that what they are really doing is putting you in *their* place, the place that they think you should be occupying. But you have the power to go where you want, and you shouldn't allow yourself to be held back by people who want to put you down. Be sensitive to the language that the people around you use. Keep an ear out as to whether they are words meant to encourage or to tear you down, even in small ways. And more important, make sure that you talk to yourself with constructive words. Some days, the voice you hear the most is the one in your own head, and its effects can be powerful. No matter how many supporters, mentors, or allies you might have, it all begins with you and the way you think about yourself. Try this on for size. Say, "I am valuable."

Associate with a Group of Like-Minded People

When I first knew I wanted to write screenplays, I enrolled in classes. If you have an area of interest, and you have already graduated from school, you should absolutely look into what kind of supplementary courses are available to you. There are even more and more courses available online that fit all kinds of schedules and budgets. I found the teachers I had extremely helpful in introducing me to some of the concepts that went into a good screenplay, and I put this information to work right away. But as much as I benefited from the instruction, it was inspiring to be around the other like-minded souls who were taking this class. Surrounding myself with people who shared common interests and goals was a great motivator. I knew in theory that I wasn't alone in my desire to write screenplays, but meeting with real live people who were struggling with the same issues and the same doubts as I was gave me a context for my own expectations. And attending classes and finishing assignments helped me establish a routine and some short-term goals that kept me on the right path.

Find a Powerful Symbol to Motivate You

Another step I took that helped me was my decision to work as a security guard on the lot of Sony Pictures Entertainment. You've probably seen it in one movie or another, but each of the studios has a huge lot where they have individual studios for filming TV shows, movies, whatever is needed. These are enormously busy spaces with people coming and going and all of the equipment of the industry. You are surrounded by the camera dollies, the Fresnel lights with their barn doors, the riser stands. These were all the concrete manifestations of where my dreams could lead. If I was ever fortunate enough to have a movie that actually went into production, these were the people who might be working on it. Remember when I said that it was a good idea to stay close to your dream even if you might not ever achieve precisely what you envision? This was an example where I kept myself close to my passion and it kept me intellectually energized as I made a living and stayed useful in any way that I could.

I know that in an earlier chapter I criticized the extent to which we value physical things over people or ideals. But I do have one confession to make and that is that I have a passion for cars. Not the model cars I work on, but the real thing. It's especially easy to feel that way in L.A., where cars are such an important part of the social network, but I've always loved them. Even when I was stupidly abusing them during my childhood in Cleveland. And you can imagine that the cars on a movie lot were the crème de la crème. There was one, a Bentley Continental Flying Spur, that stole my heart. I would tell myself that after my great success, I would be slipping into those buttery leather seats. As far out as that was—and I can assure you there's no Bentley in my driveway as I write this—it was fun to fantasize about what I could achieve if I really tried.

Persevere

Change and reinvention are hard but necessary. When do you know it's time to reinvent yourself? For me, it was when I was able to finally take my blinders off and see that I was nowhere near where I wanted to be in life. It is pretty easy to be content, but when you get out in the world and you experience as much as you can, you see beyond what was once your horizon. Your view of the world takes on a new dimension.

Every step on my journey to success was difficult. There were lots of moments when I just wanted to give up, but I heard, sometimes faintly, sometimes as a full-throated shout, that I was worth the effort. I had a value far greater than others seemed to think. The idea that I had something to prove—to myself, to all those who doubted me—helped me to keep going when I just wanted to throw my hands up in surrender and say, "You're right, I can't be anything but what your narrow-minded vision leads you to believe."

Let Others Catch Up to You

It's also important to remember that when you do reinvent yourself, some people are going to be unwilling to recognize the change and accept you for your new self. That's sometimes hard, but you need to be patient and give them time to adjust. The opposite is also true. You need to understand where you came from. When I was finally promoted to petty officer third class, I was put in charge of a small group of sailors. Many of the guys on my crew were fellow enlisted men with whom I'd previously shared rate. After my promotion, I wanted to make a good impression so that my superiors would notice me. I started off really strict with the guys and they resented me. I was trying too hard to get a good report at the expense of these sailors. Finally, after hearing the guys grumble and even come close to openly defying me, the chief petty officer of my division, Senior Chief Lawrence, took me aside and told me that I needed to remember what it was like to be in their shoes. I had to remember that in my mind I'd been reinvented but in theirs I was still a budding leader.

Inventing and reinventing yourself is one of the purest and most essential acts of control you can perform. When you feel that you are valuable, you understand that like gold, you can be melted down and cast into a new form—one of greater value, one that reveals a different facet of your essential self.

CHAPTER EIGHT

A PLACE FOR EVERYTHING AND EVERYTHING IN ITS PLACE

Now that your head is swimming with questions about where you are going in life and how you are going to get there, let's give you something for your hands to do while you are preoccupied with your bright horizons. By now you've noticed that organization is a major theme throughout these pages, whether it is organizing your wardrobe, your day, or your plans for the future. It was really in the navy that I came to appreciate organization for its positive reinforcement. There are still a couple of important areas in the life of a young man we haven't touched on that I want to tackle in *A Boy Should Know How to Tie a Tie*. These are specific actions you can take that will improve your life, make you more valuable to those around you, and give you a sense of control and stability. First, I want to talk about the place you live, whether it's a dorm room, a house, or an apartment. It's your sanctuary—the place you return to at the end of the day, where you're thinking and relaxing. And hopefully, it's a place where you entertain friends and, who knows, maybe bring a date to prepare her a meal.

The second aspect of your life is your finances. Too many of us grow up with little understanding of our finances. We just kind of let them happen and hope for the best. I don't need to tell you, this isn't the smartest way to handle things. Having spent nights out in the cold without a roof over my head on the streets of Cleveland, I can tell you that money isn't everything, but it does get you shelter, and food, and the other essentials we simply need to have. And in this economy, with its ups and downs, handling your money wisely can help you get through tough times if you ever meet unexpected circumstances. But about that house of yours . . .

Cleaning House

Growing up at the Picketts' house meant getting the job done when it came to cleaning house. When I was very young, I was only responsible for bringing the laundry down into the basement and sorting it. As I got older, new chores came my way. Every Saturday, we scrubbed the baseboards and the walls. We used a broom on all the carpets and rugs throughout the house. The thing that has stuck with me all these years is us cleaning the walls every week. The Picketts were fanatical about us not touching the walls, but we were kids, and well, you know the rest.

I wasn't crazy about cleaning—who is?—but if we were busily engaged in doing what we were supposed to, there was no chance of anything else bad happening. The fact that I relate cleaning to safety tells you how bad things could get for us. If the only thing you don't like about it is the dirt and grime, or the terrible smell of some of the cleansers, maybe you should be thankful for being a normal kid leading a normal life.

As a father, I try to do things differently than the Picketts, of course. But as my girls have gotten a little older themselves, it's time for them to take responsibility for their rooms and some of the chores around the house. If you are still living at home, it's probably time for you too, if you are not already doing it.

The Value of Clean and Neat

If clean was the order of the day at the Picketts, the navy just took it to a whole new level. The first berthing space I occupied—what the navy calls a living space onboard a ship—housed more than 100 sailors. The navy thrives on order, and the story of learning to tie a tie with which I began the book is a good example of the fundamentals of discipline and order on which the navy runs. But when I boarded my first ship, the USS *Schenectady*, I totally understood why these principles were necessary. When I was shown the berthing compartment, it looked more like a *birthing* compartment, with 100 hatchlings jammed into the smallest imaginable quarters. You couldn't have 100 young men living in that small a space if you had all their junk lying around, their towels and dirty laundry on the deck or on the racks (bed). The navy was very strict about how we kept our personal area and gear. Locker inspections were a regular and frustrating part of our weekly routine. Again, because space was limited, they didn't want you acquiring too many things and bringing them onboard. For example, you couldn't have more civilian clothing than you did navy-issue apparel. If officers discovered that you had an excess of civilian clothes during locker inspection, they would take your civilian clothes privileges away. If that happened, then when you were in port and out on liberty, you'd have to wear your uniform, something most of us didn't want to do. Liberty was a precious chance to leave your military identity behind—but you couldn't do that if you were still in uniform.

Everything we had was subject to inspection and possible confiscation. Boom boxes were popular back then and we all liked to listen to music. If during an inspection it was determined that your boom box was taking up too much space, you would be ordered to find another place for it or get rid of it. What little storage space you had been allotted needed to be devoted to the most important items: uniforms. If you lost your civilian clothes privileges because you didn't have the proper number of uniforms, you could only get them back by proving in the next sea bag inspection that you had the correct number of uniforms, socks, underwear, and so on. We all worked dirty jobs and you couldn't keep stained clothes around and count them as good. They had to be replaced. That meant buying new uniforms. As a young man, buying uniforms with your earnings was on or near the bottom of your list of priorities, but it was at the top of the navy's. A cool leather jacket versus navy dungarees? Which would you have chosen? So it was a hard lesson sometimes in setting your own priorities and making the right choices—or suffering the consequences.

I also learned some valuable lessons about frugality—more on that in the next chapter—and making do with just a small number of things. As I mentioned, I like to have a few favorite things on hand, but I've never been a pack rat. I've never even had the chance to have that luxury until much later in life. When I was in boot camp and I had to fold every T-shirt and pair of undershorts just so, with the creases perfectly perpendicular and all that, I asked myself, *What is the point of all this?* What a waste of time. I could just ball them up and throw them in a drawer. Then when I arrived back at what we called the berthing—our living quarters—and saw how little space we had, I better appreciated what the navy was doing for me. If you weren't orderly and didn't understand the old line about a place for everything and everything in its place before you entered the navy or by the time you completed basic training, you sure did in the berthing space.

Now that I'm back in civilian life, I still carry many of the navy's principles when it comes to ordering my residence. As boys, we often have the liberty of getting away with rooms that are easily classified as disaster areas. I've even heard stories about guys who could get lost in their rooms under the layers of clothes, games, magazines, electronics, and so on. Is this what your room is like? You know what, that's okay. But as we mature, as we take more control of our lives and more responsibility for ourselves and our spaces (and ultimately, as fathers, for the spaces of our children), we have to stop treating our homes like dumping grounds. There are some very practical reasons for doing this: first let's start with girls. Imagine that your friend and his girlfriend are coming over and the girlfriend is bringing her friend. You've got a thing for this chick, so this is your chance. As they walk into your place, what kind of impression does your space make on this young lady? Are you a guy who has it together, who's going places. A guy who is well groomed and neat? Does she want to spend more time in a place like yours, hanging out? Or does she walk into your space and get hit with the smell of a locker room (with a hint of dinner cooking somewhere there in the background)? You have one chance to make a first impression and that impression comes when you open your door. If you're still living at home, having a clean room matters for the same reason.

Second is health. The cleaner our spaces are, the healthier. This might not be at the top of your list, but we live in a world that has some real risks and dangers such as viruses and bacteria. Dirty, sweaty clothing, dirty bathrooms, dirty kitchen countertops are all places where these elements can thrive. Keeping things cleaned properly and stored will keep you out of harm's way whether you recognize it or not.

A boy should know how to tie a tie and he should know how to mop a floor. So let's get started.

Household Cleaning

As you know, I've perhaps had more experience in the area of household cleaning than most. Let me share some of what I've learned here and I hope you find it helpful.

1. Decide how clean is clean. Everyone's standards are different, and depending on what you can reasonably live with or how much you want to improve your standard of cleaning, number 2 below will vary. But whatever your degree of clean, clean is not dust bunnies in the corner or dirty socks under the couch. It's not visible smudges of dirt on kitchen counters or wastepaper spilling over from the basket. 'Nuff said.

2. Create a cleaning schedule. You can use the calendar on your computer or phone, or use a magnet to tack a calendar to your refrigerator door. List those tasks that should be done on a daily, weekly, biweekly, monthly, or even quarterly basis. A daily task would be something such as making your bed, doing the dishes, and cleaning stovetops and countertops. Weekly tasks include washing floors, vacuuming carpets and rugs, dusting furniture, doing the laundry, and changing the linens on your bed. Biweekly tasks could be cleaning the bathroom, cleaning the inside of the refrigerator and getting rid of older or expired food. Quarterly chores could be something like washing windows.

3. Multitask. When talking on the phone with a friend, identify one or two tasks that you can reasonably do while talking.

4. Apply the sooner-rather-than-later rule. If you spill something, notice an empty glass lying around, or whatever, take care of it immediately. Messes are created when you allow things to pile up. No one wants to do the dishes when they've been stacked up for a week and have hardened food on them.

Generally, a few minutes a weekday and an hour or two maximum on the weekend should be enough time to keep most places in good working order. Just as I learned in the navy, a little preventive and regular maintenance is better than having to do a major overhaul. You can reduce the amount of stress in your life and won't be running around like a crazy person whenever company is coming over if you do things regularly and don't let stuff pile up.

A good resource for how to do many of these cleaning tasks is a book called *Clean Like a Man* by Tom McNulty. You can even buy *Clean Like a Man* as an e-book now so it won't clutter your shelves.

Here's a list of the basic supplies you should have on hand for each task.

Dusting Supplies
Cleaning cloths
Dust mop or vacuum cleaner and dusting attachment
Dusting spray and/or furniture polish

Trash Supplies
Trash cans
Trash can liners
Recycling bins

General Surface Supplies
All-purpose cleaner
Kitchen cleaner or wipes
Bathroom cleaner or wipes
Sponges
Paper towels
Scrubbers
Gloves

Special Surface Supplies
Oven cleaner
Stone cleaner (for something like granite countertops)

Dish soap
Dishwasher detergent
Wood polish
Upholstery spot remover
Leather cleaner
Laundry soap
Laundry stain remover
Laundry additives (fabric softener)
Toilet bowl cleaner
Soft scrubbing cleaner
Air freshener
Glass cleaner
Bleach
Silver or metal polish

Floor Cleaning Supplies
Broom
Dustpan
Mop
Mop bucket
Mopping solution
Floor polish

Storage and Organizing Supplies
Storage containers
Labels or labelmaker
Filing system

This might sound like a lot, but it all should easily fit into a utility closet and under the kitchen sink. Having the right tools on hand is half the challenge (and half the excuse when you don't do it because you don't have the right stuff), so go out and get these supplies and create a schedule you can live with.

I also recommend that you listen to music when you are working on household chores. A little Earth, Wind & Fire or Jay-Z can put a little tempo into your vacuuming and make the time go quicker.

Cleaning Up Your Finances

As a young man, I knew just two things about money: I didn't have much of it, and I wanted more. I was trapped in a life of financial uncertainty and I didn't like it. I told myself that one day, I would have enough money so that I didn't have those concerns. That kind of worry was very taxing (one of those money words again!) on me psychologically, physically, and spiritually. If your financial affairs are not sound, then you lack the platform from which you can grow your life to greater things. As kids, of course, we are not responsible for our financial lives, and it can be very trying if the people in charge in your life are not on top of theirs. But you can always try to do for yourself and ultimately, you will be responsible for yourself. Much of the advice below is directed at those of you who do pay your own bills and run your financial life. Especially if you were raised in an environment where these issues were not properly addressed, it's easy to try to ignore or avoid them. That's the way many men handle their business affairs, but it's not the way you'll handle yours.

Here are some tips on how to stay in control of income, bills, and taxes:

• Save all your credit card receipts in one place. A box or file folder is a great place to store this month's credit card receipts, and will give you quick access to compare them to your statement when it arrives. You should keep all receipts at least until you have verified that the charges on your bill are correct. Create a "Receipts to Keep" folder for receipts for items that may need to be returned or that have a warranty or service plan in effect.

- Organize your bill paying. Set up a regular time and place to pay bills each month. A good rule of thumb is to coordinate it with your pay schedule. If you are paid on the fifteenth and thirtieth, make plans to pay bills at those same times each month. If it makes it easier, you can log your due dates on a calendar. As bills arrive, organize them into "To Be Paid" folders and when you pay them, document payment on the statement and file under "Paid." Paying bills online can be a great time-saver. Whether you use your own financial institution or pay through the vendor's Web site, you can often schedule the payments to occur on the day of your choosing. Be sure to jot down the confirmation number as proof of payment. Some institutions even reward you with savings for paying online.

- Pay off credit cards. Make a log with each of your credit card and credit accounts, and list the outstanding balance for each. Set up a schedule to pay off the ones with the highest interest rates first. When that one is paid off, apply that money to the next card until all balances are paid. Avoid using credit cards to charge more than you can reasonably pay off at the end of the month. Use debit cards to pay with money directly withdrawn from your bank account instead of money you are borrowing with interest.

- Balance your checking account. At least twice a month, reconcile your bank statement to the bank's records. This can be done in just a few minutes online, checking off what has cleared your account and making sure you have accounted for any of those debit card purchases or ATM transactions.

- Review your insurance policies. January is an excellent time to review all insurance policies to make sure you're covered properly. If you have one, review your life insurance policy to ensure it provides adequate coverage for your family. You can save money by raising your deductibles on auto and homeowners (or renters) insurance. Every few years, shop rates, comparing policies point for point.

- Organize for your taxes. While you're pulling together information to file last year's taxes, note which categories have the most activity. Make specific folders for such categories as out-of-pocket medical and drug costs, work-related expenses such as travel/mileage if not reimbursed, educational costs, and so on. Designate one location for all tax information and keep up with filing regularly. Next year, the tax preparation process will be much easier because all the records and receipts have been kept together.

- Shred. Purge old files and shred the contents to protect yourself from identity theft. Keep a shredder near your desk and deal with incoming mail immediately. While you should check with your accountant about how long financial records should be retained, a good rule of thumb is to keep tax records and credit card statements for seven years. Keep pay stubs until you get your year-end tax forms, and keep key banking information permanently.

- Check your credit report. Consumers can request a free copy of their credit report from each of the three bureaus each year. Set up a regular schedule to get reports from www.annualcreditreport.com. A good rule of thumb is to get the report from one bureau in January, another in May, and a third in September. Notify the bureaus immediately if you find any errors or unusual activity, such as accounts you did not open. Good credit is important when it's time to buy that first house.

- Compile a list of all your account numbers, passwords, and other important financial information so that if you are incapacitated in an accident (or worse), you won't leave behind a tangled mess for your family members to sort out.

Saving Money

As I write this, we are in the middle of one of the most serious economic crises in recent American history, if not longer. One of the key contributors to this problem is that Americans as a whole have one of the lowest saving rates in history. Simply put, far too many of us are spending more than we make, relying on various lines of credit—charge cards, home mortgages, auto loans—to allow us to have today what we really can't afford. We are living well beyond our means, buying today what we likely couldn't really afford until many, many tomorrows have gone by. I'm not against owning a home or a car or other nice things, but being realistic about what you can and can't afford is important. As a nation, we're learning what happens when you don't clean up your financial act or take care of the tangled mess that has resulted from our collective desire to have it all now.

As you well know from the previous chapter, I believe that developing control is important, and taking control of your spending is an excellent place to learn some valuable life lessons. I also told you that I grew up as a keen observer, and that's a skill you need to get your financial house in order. How do you know how much money you're spending? You probably have a vague idea, but if it consists of checking your account balance when you make an ATM withdrawal, you need some more precise measures of keeping track of expenses.

What many financial experts suggest is that you spend a week keeping track of every dollar you spend during that time period. You can do this simply by dedicating a small notebook to writing down all of your cash expenditures during the course of a day. If you stop for a burger somewhere, write down the amount you paid. Alternatively, you can keep all of your receipts and tally them at the end of the day. One problem with this is that if you slide a few quarters into a soda or candy machine, you don't get a receipt. You need to track *all* your cash spending. You might wonder now about your noncash expenses—paying bills, and so on. We'll deal with those more-or-less regular expenses in a bit. As far as credit card and debit card spending, you should keep track of those as well. Remember how, earlier, I asked you to keep track of just how you were spending your time? As you plan to create that kind of journal to get an overview of where you spend you time, now you will keep track of where you spend your money. I bet you find both of these exercises eye opening, and in the long haul, the effort you put in will be well worth the time. (I'm going to ask you to track one last thing in the next chapter.)

Information Analysis

I'm pretty sure that you're going to be surprised by what you find. When you take a good look, money just seems to flow out of your pockets. Once you've identified total expenditures, take a look at each expense and see if you can find a category for it. Note how much money you spend on food, entertainment, gas, and so on. The point of this exercise is not just to track parts of your personal budget, but to make you aware of how much money you are spending versus how much you are bringing in. Most of us are paid weekly or every two weeks. When you realize what you spend money on on a daily basis, you can probably see why Americans (and maybe you) save so little.

The Budget

Michael Farr is the author of the book *A Million Is Not Enough*. He is the founder and president of the investment firm Farr, Miller &

Washington in Washington, D.C. His book is directed at people who are smart enough to plan their retirement and suggests that an individual today needs a million dollars in savings at retirement to live comfortably. A million dollars! It seems like a fortune when you are pulling in a paycheck in the hundreds or low thousands. But the trick is starting early, and setting aside even a few dollars today can make a big difference twenty, thirty, or forty years down the road. And the habits you start now—like saving and balancing your accounts—will last a lifetime. The bottom line is that it is never too early to develop good financial habits. Mr. Farr works with some wealthy clients who probably don't fit your preconceived notions of what "wealthy" looks like.

I spoke with Mr. Farr and he said, "One of the things that impresses me about so-called smaller investors is the discipline they bring to the table. These people have accumulated a healthy amount of savings and investment income through hard work and by applying one 'simple' rule: They live within their means. They have nice but not extravagant homes, they drive ten-year-old cars, they pay cash for most things, and they enjoy what they have and don't spend a whole lot of time wishing they had more than that. Instead, they have a vision of what they want their lives to be like, develop a plan for how to get there, make changes as necessary (not just on a whim), and prepare for the worst while hoping for—and taking steps to insure—that they will experience the best."

Mr. Farr added that these people were among his happiest clients. If you want to know more about the people Mr. Farr is talking about, a very good book called *The Millionaire Next Door* can be found at your local library. It is filled with stories of people you would think are the most unlikely candidates to be millionaires, based on what they own and how they appear, but they actually are. It also gives you good advice about the strategies they employed to "get rich." Many of the lessons in that book are similar to these five points Mr. Farr gave me as financial advice to young people:

1. Learn the value of a dollar early, both what effort it takes to earn one and what you really "earn" when you spend one.
2. Understand the value of saving and the magic of compound interest.
3. Create a vision for where you want to be financially, develop a plan to get there, and have the discipline to stick with the plan.
4. Live within your means.

And perhaps most important . . .
5. Enjoy what you have.

How to Develop a Plan

According to Mr. Farr and others, one of the first things that you need to do is to track your expenses even more carefully than I suggested earlier. You need to know what point you're starting from before you can decide what directions to take to get to your destination. That entails developing a budget, which is little more than tracking what comes in and what goes out each month. Obviously, if you have more going out than you have coming in, you're in trouble. Here's a typical budget tracking sheet you can use. Leave blank any areas that don't apply to you. A tracking sheet like this can help you as your financial life evolves.

MONTHLY BUDGET SCHEDULE

	January	February	March	Monthly Average
INCOME DESCRIPTION				
Wages	$	$	$	$
Interest and dividends	$	$	$	$
Miscellaneous	$	$	$	$
TOTAL INCOME	$	$	$	$
EXPENSE DESCRIPTION				
Housing				
Mortgage payment or Rent	$	$	$	$
Home repairs	$	$	$	$
Insurance	$	$	$	$
Utilities				
Electricity	$	$	$	$
Gas	$	$	$	$
Telephone bill	$	$	$	$
Water	$	$	$	$
Cell phone	$	$	$	$
Transportation				
Auto insurance	$	$	$	$
Auto payment	$	$	$	$
Gasoline	$	$	$	$
Auto maintenance	$	$	$	$
Bus or subway/train	$	$	$	$
Food				
Groceries	$	$	$	$
Necessary outside meals	$	$	$	$
Household				
Cleaning expenses	$	$	$	$
Other upkeep	$	$	$	$

	January	February	March	Monthly Average
Personal Care				
Beauty shop or barber	$	$	$	$
Clothing	$	$	$	$
Laundry and dry cleaning	$	$	$	$
Entertainment and recreation				
Cable TV	$	$	$	$
Internet access	$	$	$	$
Club dues	$	$	$	$
Subscriptions	$	$	$	$
Movie rentals	$	$	$	$
Games	$	$	$	$
Activities	$	$	$	$
Restaurants	$	$	$	$
Vacations	$	$	$	$
Health				
Health insurance	$	$	$	$
Life insurance	$	$	$	$
Medical and dental out-of-pocket	$	$	$	$
Charity	$	$	$	$
Gifts	$	$	$	$
Debt payments				
Home equity	$	$	$	$
Credit card payments	$	$	$	$
Other debt payments	$	$	$	$
All other	$	$	$	$
TOTAL EXPENSES	$	$	$	$
CASH (SHORT)/EXTRA	$	$	$	$

By tracking your income and expenses over three months, you will get a better sense of your spending and savings patterns. As you did with your informal weekly check of spending, look at each category and take note of the patterns you've developed. If, for example, you do a quick calculation and find that nearly a quarter of your income is spent on entertainment, and you are saving nothing each month, you need to cut back some in that area.

Becoming more consciously aware of what you spend is probably the most important step you can take in cleaning up your finances. Most of us go around blindly spending and only take notice of it when we get to the end of a pay period and realize (too late) that we don't have enough to cover our expenses. That's not a good spot to be in. We'll talk about what you can do when you are in this spot later in the chapter. For now, we need to talk about the difference between what you earn and what you spend from a slightly more sophisticated (and important) perspective.

Knowing Your Net Worth

I started this book and the discussion of your value as an individual by talking about the dollar value placed on my body and what the state of Ohio gave to the people who cared for me. In the real world of personal finance, there's a calculation you can do that is used as part of a formula for determining your credit worthiness. It is called your net worth. In business terms, net worth is calculated by subtracting your liabilities (what you owe) from your assets (what you have). The single figure called net worth is the amount that would be left if you took everything you possessed and sold it to pay off your debts. Here's a simple chart that you can use to determine your net worth.

CATEGORY	CURRENT VALUE
ASSETS:	
Cash in savings accounts	$
Cash in checking accounts	$
Certificates of deposit (CDs)	$
Cash on hand	$
Money market accounts	$
Money owed to me (rent deposits, etc.)	$
Cash value of life insurance	$
Savings bonds (current value)	$
Stocks	$
Bonds	$
Mutual funds	$
Vested value of stock options	$
Other investments	$
Individual retirement accounts (IRAs)	$
Keogh accounts	$
401(k) or 403(b) accounts	$
Other retirement plans	$
Market value of home	$
Market value of other real estate	$
Blue book value of cars/trucks, boats, planes, other vehicles	$
Jewelry	$
Collectibles	$
Furnishings and other personal property	$
Other	$
TOTAL ASSETS	$
LIABILITIES:	
Mortgages	$

CATEGORY	CURRENT VALUE
Car loans	$
Bank loans	$
Student loans	$
Home equity loans	$
Other loans	$
Credit card balances	$
Real estate taxes owed	$
Income taxes owed	$
Other taxes owed	$
Other debts	$
TOTAL LIABILITIES	$
NET WORTH (total assets less total liabilities)	$

I hope it's clear that you want this to be a positive number. Determining the value of your bank accounts is easy. What objects are worth is a little bit trickier, so your net worth is always kind of an estimate. Despite that, I hope you realize that it is important to either have a positive number as your net worth or understand that your negative number (you owe more than you own) is a result of having a large loan on a house or something of great value.

Reality Check

I know that some of you are thinking at this point, *Hey, I'm a kid or teen. My parents take care of me financially. Why do I need to know any of this?* Well, the fact is that if your parents don't teach you some of these lessons, chances are your school won't, and you could end up learning the hard way. I was in that boat (pun intended) when I was in the navy. I had little financial expertise or experience. I was earning a salary, and as I said before, the navy was basically taking care of my other needs—housing and food. Sound like your situation? Well, when I was out of the navy's nest and sailing on my own, I quickly realized I had a lot to learn about managing money. I'll spare you the details, but I had my own share of financial downturns. They weren't too bad because I'm a cautious person by nature, but I also saw lots of my friends and acquaintances struggling with credit card debt and all the rest. Living from paycheck to paycheck and wondering if you're going to have enough money to pay all your bills is not only not fun—it is very unwise.

Why Does Net Worth Matter?

Your net worth gives you a rough sense of what your credit rating might be. In the United States three companies (Experian, Equifax, and TransUnion) keep track of your financial data and calculate a number that reflects your credit worthiness—in other words, the number represents how good of a credit risk you are. When you want to take out a loan, get a credit card, and so on, banks and credit card companies will get your rating from these agencies and determine whether or not they will give you a loan, and at what interest rate. A lot more goes into your credit score than your net worth.

What's Important
- Your payment history
- The amount of debt you owe
- What type of debt it is (car or home loans, credit cards, store charges)
- How much new credit you have and your credit limits
- How long your credit history is
- The amount of debt you have in relation to your total credit limits

Of Lesser Weight
- Education level
- Home ownership
- Stable address
- Years of employment

Your Rights

According to federal law, you are entitled to receive one free credit report each year from each of those three agencies. Getting one of those each year should be on your financial schedule. Knowing where you stand and why is important. Often, errors are made in these reports and it's important that you be aware of what's on your record so that you can challenge those errors. Also, you need to understand why you were turned down for some form of credit and why you were assigned a particular interest rate for any credit you are eligible to receive. Go to www.ftc.gov/freereports for more information on how to get these reports, dispute errors, and more.

Credit Counseling

If you do find that you have gotten yourself into the position where you have too much credit card debt, are unable to make timely payments on your house, your car, or otherwise need help in controlling spending and increasing savings, there are a number of organizations you can turn to for help. The worst thing you can do is to ignore the problem and hope it will go away. Playing the credit card game—taking out new lines of credit to help pay off other credit card debt—is a no-win proposition. You won't ever get out of debt that way. Credit can be a good thing, but it can also be an evil thing.

I've seen many examples to prove this point, but here's one from about.com and its financial pages that I'll briefly summarize.

You want to buy a $2,000 television. You have a credit card that charges 18 percent a month, which is pretty high, but they sent you an offer saying that you only have to pay forty dollars a month on the $2,000 line of credit they will "give" you. You decide to use the card to pay for the TV and pay only the forty dollars minimum the credit card company was so generous to give you. It will take you thirty years to pay off that TV. You will pay $5,000 in interest on that TV, bringing its actual cost to $7,000. If, instead of paying that forty dollars a month, you had saved that amount and put it in an investment that earned 8 percent interest per year (such as stocks), at the end of the same time period (thirty years) your forty-dollars-a-month investment would be worth $64,000, of which $46,000 would be interest!

If you've gotten yourself into a position where you need credit counseling, there are a number of nonprofit agencies you can turn to. It's important to note that these companies won't charge you for their services. Many other for-profit credit counseling agencies are out there, and a number of them make it seem like it won't cost you anything for their help, but they do charge for their services. Be very cautious and make sure that you understand fully what you're getting yourself into.

There are so many of these agencies, nonprofit and for-profit alike, and they vary from one geographic area to another, that I can't really give you suggestions on which ones to consult. What I can tell you is no matter which one you find (either by searching the phone book or the Internet for credit counseling services), you should also contact your local Better Business Bureau to see if the agencies record is a good one. You can do this online by going to www.bbb.com. You will be asked for your zip code and then you will be taken to your local Better Business Bureau's Web site. Once there, you can type in the name of the agency and you will be given the assessment you are asking for. While that may sound like a lot of effort, look back at the cost of credit example earlier.

I can say that for downloads of a budget-tracking worksheet like the one I provided earlier and lots of other good advice, you can go to www.consumercredit.com/budget-sheet.htm. American Consumer Credit Counseling is a nonprofit agency, and on their Web site they have many good resources that are free, including that budget worksheet and others. Read the Frequently Asked Questions (FAQ) section to learn more about their services and the nominal fee that they do charge. That's right—nonprofit doesn't mean *free*.

Consumer Reports, The Motley Fool, *Money* magazine, MSN, *Kiplinger*, and *Forbes*, among many other magazines, financial networks, and organizations have Web sites that also offer great advice on all matters of personal finance including credit.

Putting It All Together

So far this whole financial chat has been a bit of a downer. Let me show you how you can put all of this information into a positive light. I've said before that I love cars, and getting a car for the first time is a real step toward manhood. So let's talk about some of the thinking and steps you might go through to make a wise choice in purchasing your first new car. (I'm going to use buying a new car as an example because the interest rates on loans generally vary less than they do for used cars. In general, it's always a good idea to buy used. Cars depreciate [go down in value] very quickly. The rule of thumb is to pay cash for what depreciates. Also, by buying used, you can let someone else suffer the effect of that depreciating asset. Cars lose their value more quickly in the first few years than they do down the line.)

If you're going to live within your means, you will have to decide what it is that you can afford. Most likely that means that your fantasy of owning a Ferrari, a Porsche, or an even more exotic car like a Lamborghini is out of the question. That doesn't mean that you have to settle for an old beat up whip or a boring family sedan, though. Let's say that you determine that there's room in your budget for $375 a month for a car. You start to look at cars that you might enjoy owning. You're smart enough to realize that the amount you allocated for a car needs to include more than just the car payment. You also have to account for insurance, maintenance, and fuel. That limits the field a bit. You want a fuel-efficient and reliable car that's not too high-performance. Why the last of those? Insurance rates for younger drivers are higher than they are for anyone else. The highest rates are often assigned to vehicles with the most horsepower because young people too often can't resist using that horsepower in inappropriate ways. As a result, they get into a lot of accidents, which increases the rates assigned to those cars. Remember, insurers don't just look at you and your driving record, they look at other people in a similar age group as well as the type of vehicle and its history of claims.

You still want to have a fun-to-drive car, and you understand it's important to balance that desire with your need for something efficient and reliable. (For now we'll ignore the question of safety because most new cars have an abundance of safety features.) You do some looking around and some reading. You've heard that Toyota has a great reputation for reliability and their cars are reasonably efficient. You look on their Web site and as much as you might want an SUV, they are awfully expensive and not so fuel efficient. That leaves you with a few choices: the Prius, the Corolla, the Yaris, and the Matrix. All pretty boring choices. You're environmentally minded and the Prius being a hybrid is a plus, but still, the car is not attractive. Same with the others. Too bland. You've read some car magazines and you know about Toyota's other youth-oriented brand, the Scion, so you check out their Web site.

You click to go on Scion's site and you realize that hey, Toyota isn't just for conservative family types. They do produce a line of cars that you wouldn't be embarrassed to be seen in. This site is clearly directed at younger people, and so are the cars. They definitely have some funky design things going on with their xB and xD models, but even with all that funk, they're still a station wagon. A kind of bathtub-meets-delivery-van kind of wagon. You're all for utility, but it's the tC that really catches your eye. Much more sporty, and you discover that it has 161 horsepower and still gets 27 miles per gallon on the highway. And even better, Toyota is offering free maintenance for the first two scheduled services. Better yet, the base price is $17,670. You're no math genius, but you figure that has to fit into your budget.

You go through the process of building your own purchase online, choosing the color and options you want. You're smart enough to know that it's safer to do this online: if you go to the showroom unarmed with information, you might get swept up by emotion and a savvy car salesman and not get the best deal. The other advantage of the online build-your-own feature is that you can choose all different combinations of options and packages and price them out to see how they fit in your budget. Even better, when you're done building it (creating your vision) you can price it out and find what it will cost you to finance it. You don't have enough money to pay cash, so you are going to have to get a loan. The Scion Web site has its own loan calculator, and you can also find many easy-to-use ones on the Web. They're all pretty similar. They ask you the amount you are going to finance. That means that you will put up some cash as a down payment. You have $5,000 saved for a car, plus you have a standing offer of another $5,000 for your current car from a private buyer. That's $10,000, but you're not sure you want to use all of it.

The next thing you do is calculate various scenarios. You need to know what the typical finance rate is for new cars. One great site for this is bankrate.com. Not only do they present a daily list of the average rates for new cars, they have a loan calculator you can use to determine what your monthly payment might be. As I write this in August 2009, bankrate.com says that the average new car loan interest rate for a forty-eight-month payback schedule is 7.23 percent. We're going to assume for this example that you don't have the best credit rating because you don't have a long credit history and the best rate that you can get as a result is 8 percent. The car you've configured costs $21,316. That's before taxes and other fees, but we'll use that number anyway so that you can get the general idea.

That car has a few options. There were a lot more you would have liked to have, but you did choose some appearance and performance parts—a rear deck spoiler, special sport wheels, and an anti-sway bar. You wanted to upgrade the sound system, but you know that you can get a better deal and have more options if you go to a car stereo store instead.

You try out some possible payment options based on this price. First, you see what your monthly payment would be if you used $5,000 as a down payment. That means that you would be financing $16,316. You enter that number, select forty-eight months as the term (length) of the loan, and enter 8 percent as your estimated interest rate. Yikes. Your payment would be $398.32 a month for forty-eight months. That's $23 over your budget. Your first thought (and it's not a particularly good one) is to extend the loan out for another year so that you can get under your budget number. (More later on why that doesn't make good sense.) Doing that would reduce your payment to $330.83 a month for 60 months. *Cool*, you think. That's below the $375 you budgeted. But that doesn't account for insurance and gas. Maintenance is taken care of for the first 10,000 miles, so you can delete that from your calculation.

Next you go to Geico.com and Progressive.com to get a free

insurance quote. Those aren't the only two insurers who offer that service, but they are two of the more popular options. You fill in all the details and receive a quote for $1,000 a year. That's $83.33 a month. Add that to the payment and you're back over your original budget estimate by $106.65 a month.

As tempting as it is to just say, "What's $23?" When you figure in the cost of insurance, you're now $106.65 over your budget and you also know that you have to put fuel in your car. That's going to put you even more over budget, but just to carry this scenario out to its end, you do some additional research. You Google "average gas prices" and you find out that the government has a Web site, www .eia.doe.gov/oil_gas/petroleum/data_publications/wrgp/mogas_ home_page.html, that tracks the average price of a gallon of gas in regions all across the country. You learn that for you in the Midwest, that average is $2.51 for regular grade as of August 7, 2009. The site also shows you what the prices were one and two weeks prior to that date. Great information to have.

Next you need to figure out how fuel efficient the Scion tC is. The Scion Web site said that it got 20 mpg in the city and 27 mpg on the highway. You're going to be doing a mix of city and highway driving. Your commute to work is twenty miles each way, so that's forty miles round trip times five days a week, which means you'll be driving 200 miles a week commuting at a minimum. You figure another 100 miles to account for errands and weekends and you're at 300 miles a week. You have no idea how to determine what your actual mileage will be, but someone else has done that work for you. If you go to www.fueleconomy.gov, you can get real data on thousands of cars. You enter your car in the search field and you find out a whole bunch of useful information.

Fuel Type	Regular
MPG (city)	20

MPG (highway)	27
MPG (combined)	23
Fuel Economics:	
Cost to drive 25 miles	$2.65
Fuel to drive 25 miles	1.09 gal
Cost of a fill-up	$31.84
Miles on a tank	300 miles
Tank size	14.5 gal
Annual Fuel Cost	$1,592

Great, they've done the calculations for you. You will need approximately one 14.5 tank of gas per week. They used $2.65 per gallon to come up with costs of a tank and the yearly consumption, but you found out that for your region, the cost would be $2.51. Knowing that gas prices could go up, you decide to use that higher figure. If the annual fuel cost is $1,592 then the monthly cost of gas is one-twelfth of that figure, $132.66. Now the true cost of owning that vehicle comes into play. You're at $614.31 for a forty-eight month loan. Even if you extend the payments out to sixty months, in either case, that's way over your budget. You'd be paying $546.82.

Now what? Your next thought is to see how much your cost of ownership per month will be if you use all of that $10,000 down payment money. Here's how that scenario looks.

Amount financed = $11,316 (purchase price of $21,316-$10,000 down)
Term of loan = 60 months
Interest rate = 8%
Monthly payment = $229.45
Total monthly cost of ownership = $445.44

Still over that budget, but you've gotten closer. You know that you'll be able to get the car for less than sticker price, so that will reduce the amount you finance by some, but you also realize that all those options you added are going to add greatly to the cost. You decide to see what it will cost you for the base model with no options, using your $5,000 and $10,000 down scenarios. You realize that when you subtract $5,000 from the base price of $17,670 the amount you'd have to finance is higher than what you just figured out. That's not going to work, so you do the calculations based on the $10,000 down.

Base price: $17,670
Down payment: $10,000
Amount financed: $7,670
Term of loan: 60 months
Interest rate: 8 percent
Monthly payment: $155.52
Total monthly car costs: $155.52 + $83.33 (insurance)
        + $132.66 (fuel) = $371.51

You're under budget! You congratulate yourself for that. You realize that you can afford this car. You may not get all the equipment on it that you want, but that's part of becoming an adult. Making compromises, readjusting priorities, and so on. You also realize something else: what a difference it makes if you have a substantial down payment. Saving your money and not financing a huge amount makes a big difference. What you might fail to realize is a couple of other things. By adding that additional year of payments, you were able to "afford" that car. Or were you?

Let's run the numbers based on a forty-eight-month payment plan. Your payment would be $187.25. The other costs are the same and your total monthly car expense would therefore be $403.24. That's $28.24 over your budgeted amount. Which would be better to do: Go over your budget by $28.24 a month or extend the loan by a year and stay under budget? Here's where Mr. Farr's suggestion that you learn the true cost of spending a dollar comes into play. Remember when I said that your thought about getting a sixty-month loan wasn't a good one? Well, it's true that you were able to get under budget that way, but let's look at what the true cost of that choice would be and how for any purchase the length of a loan increases the amount you have to pay over time:

Number of Months		Monthly Payment		Total Cost
60	X	$155.52	=	$9,331.20
48	X	$187.25	=	$8,988.00
36	X	$240.35	=	$8,652.60

You would have saved nearly $350 by choosing to go with a forty-eight-month loan and $679 by going with a thirty-six-month loan. That may not sound like a lot of money, but you need to consider how much money you might have earned in interest by saving that amount over a four- or five-year period. Interest compounds: That means that you earn interest on the interest you've already been "paid." That adds up quickly. If you'd taken that $350 ($29.16 a month) you would have saved that year and invested it in something that earned a conservative 8 percent return you would have earned $2.33 in interest that first year. Add that number to your original balance, and do that again and again for, let's say, fifty years until you retire and that small amount balloons to $1,338.49.

In other words, you need to have a long-term and a short-term vision. Yes, that initial amount seems small, but when you think as a saver and not as a spender, you realize what can happen to small amounts over the long haul. If small amounts get bigger, then large amounts get even bigger even faster. Let's say you decided to not buy that car. Instead, you took the $5,000 you saved and invested it, and told yourself that in three years you were going to buy a new car. You'd have an additional $1,300 to use as a down payment.

Let's review a few of the key points this car-buying example raises.

- Do your homework before buying anything.
- Determine what your budget allows.
- Factor in all the costs of ownership.
- Understand the additional costs of getting credit.
- Take out credit or loans for the shortest term possible for items that will decrease in value.
- Be prepared to make priority-based decisions based on fact and not emotion—know what you want and what you truly need.

I hope you understand that this is just an example. As much as possible I tried to make the numbers realistic. A lot of variables go into the cost of a car, insurance, gas, and so on, but the thought process I took you through is a good one. There are a number of good car buying guides available. Among the ones that will help you through the various stages are those from *Consumer Reports*, cars.com, and Edmunds.com. They can assist you in all facets of car buying and take some of the pain away when making this major purchase. Edmunds also has a price guide service and lots of reviews of cars, actual dealers' cost versus sticker price, and so on.

Knowledge is valuable. You are valuable. Put the two together and you have increased your power exponentially.

An African American Perception

Perception is reality. In other words, what you think is true is true for you no matter what the "truth" (factually supported) really is. In the African American community, there has long been the perception that African American men aren't keeping up their responsibilities. We are imprisoned in disproportionate numbers, don't support our women financially and spiritually, and achieve academically at a lower rate than African American women. Generally, finding a dependable partner for women is a challenge. I spoke earlier about the irony of being called no-account and that's the perception that some women have of African American men.

I can't and won't go into all the complex issues contained in this perception. It's out there, and because of that, it's important that any young black male reading this do whatever you can to make sure that perception doesn't apply to you. So much of our popular culture revolves around bling and money and status that you may feel you have to obtain the kind of ostentatious displays of wealth that are featured in music videos. The truth is that just as most women are not interested in finding movie stars, athletes, or recording artists, all you need to do (as I pointed out with your self and your clothes) is to keep your finances neat and clean. You don't have to earn the big bucks, drive the nice ride, or treat your girl to every extravagance. But being in debt, spending recklessly, and having your financial house in ruins are sure tickets to loneliness. This is true no matter the color of your skin.

Learning to be financially responsible while you're young will help you develop the habits that keep you clear of credit counseling services and likely keep you from disappointing your partner. Keeping your literal house and your financial house as neat and clean and as comfortable as possible is an important part of what it means to be a man.

I was fortunate in some ways that the navy served as my family, but they also took care of a lot of financial issues for me. Once I left the navy and lived apart from that family, I had to learn about a lot of these matters. There are lots of good resources available online and in bookstores about budgeting and investing and all the other personal finance topics. One of the real problems that many young people get into is overspending and incurring credit card debt. Good financial planning and discipline are very important, and how to handle money is something that not all families are comfortable talking about. I know that I wasn't alone in finding myself in a confusing place dealing with taxes, insurance, and bills. Taking responsibility for those things is a part of building your image and increasing your self-esteem and value.

CHAPTER NINE

YOU ARE WHAT YOU EAT

A few weeks ago, I went to see my doctor for a physical. Nearing fifty, I'm at the age when it makes sense to have a yearly checkup and keep a closer eye on what's going on with my body. Along with the exam, a nurse drew some blood. Every time they do that, I'm always surprised by how thin and watery blood is. I know that it carries all the nutrients our bodies need, and realizing such an important substance is so watery always makes me pause. Shouldn't it be thick, like ketchup or pasta sauce?

One of the concerns my doctor had was with my cholesterol levels. Previous tests had shown that one aspect of my cholesterol, LDL, was too high. I'm sure you've heard plenty about cholesterol on countless TV ads—we all do. But in case you don't know, cholesterol is essentially fat in your bloodstream. LDL cholesterol (low density lipoprotein) is considered bad because it can accumulate in your arteries and slow or stop the flow of blood to important organs such as the brain and the heart. Sounds like bad stuff, right? High density lipoprotein (HDL) is the so-called good cholesterol. We need this type of cholesterol in our system because it helps to carry the LDL out of our bodies via the liver. When you get your cholesterol levels checked as an adult, you will receive a score for HDL, LDL, and total cholesterol. For total cholesterol a score below 200 means that you are at relatively low risk for a heart attack.

A person's LDL, or bad cholesterol, should be at a level between 100 and 130. Mine was at 150, considered borderline high but not that bad. When I was tested again a year later, I expected that number to go down. I eat sensibly, some would say very healthfully, and I try to exercise regularly. I use a stair climber for forty-five minutes daily and I recently returned to doing the kind of calisthenics—jumping jacks, sit-ups, and push-ups—that had been a part of my navy physical training. I hadn't let myself go completely, but as a writer, I wasn't as physically active as I had been.

The Heart of the Matter

I know that as you're sitting there reading this, you're thinking that you're nowhere near my age and what I'm going through has nothing to do with you. Well, just as it's an important part of your financial health to start thinking and acting early, now is the time to start thinking about your physical health, especially if you haven't been treating yourself as well as you should be. You can have all the money in the world, but if your body fails you, it's hard to enjoy life's riches. I included this story and this section because there is an epidemic of obesity in this country, and the African American community of which I am a part is being hit particularly hard. What is obesity? According the standards developed by the National Institutes of Health (NIH), obesity is defined as a body mass index (BMI) equal to or greater than 30. Essentially your BMI is a figure that you calculate using your height and weight. It gives you a rough idea of how much fat you are carrying on your body.

You can find several online sources for charts and calculators that ask you to enter information and will factor your BMI for you. One of them is at www.nhlbisupport.com/bmi. It asks you to enter your height and weight and then it gives you your BMI. Here's a break-down done by the NIH that shows healthy and unhealthy BMIs.

Underweight = less than 18.5
Normal weight = 18.5–24.9
Overweight = 25–29.9
Obese = 30 or greater

I don't think I have to tell you that being overweight is bad for you, but here are some of the potential consequences: diabetes, heart disease, stroke, and cancer. Those are among the leading causes of death in this country. Think about your own life and your own family. How many people have you lost in your family or your community to one of those conditions? How many people in your family currently have or have had one of those conditions?

The Fat Facts

According to the Centers for Disease Control, only one state in America, Colorado, has an obesity rate of less than 20 percent. When I came across that fact, I was astonished. Here in California, where I live, that rate is 23 percent. Put another way, nearly one in four people in California is obese. The worse state is Mississippi, where nearly one in three people is obese.

For African Americans, the news is even worse. African Americans have an obesity rate 50 percent higher than whites. African Americans have a nationwide obesity rate of 35.7 percent with the men's percentage at 31.6 percent and women's at 39.2 percent.

It's Not Just Affecting Old People

It would be easy to dismiss this trend as part of an aging population. Unfortunately for you, that's not true. Look at these two charts from the CDC showing the trend in obesity among young people. The first is for young people of all races:

PREVALENCE OF OBESITY AMONG U.S. CHILDREN AND ADOLESCENTS

(Aged 2–19 Years)

Survey Periods	1976–1980	1988–1994	1999–2002	2003–2006
Ages 2 through 5	5.0%	7.2%	10.3%	12.4%
Ages 6 through 11	6.5%	11.3%	15.8%	17.0%
Ages 12 through 19	5.0%	10.5%	16.1%	17.6%

This next chart shows the trend for young people broken down by race:

ADOLESCENT BOYS PREVALENCE OF OBESITY BY RACE/ETHNICITY

(Aged 12–19 Years)

Survey Periods	1988–1994	2003–2006
Non-Hispanic white	11.6%	17.3%
Non-Hispanic black	10.7%	18.5%
Mexican American	14.1%	22.1%

The numbers are frightening—roughly two out of ten young people between the ages of twelve and nineteen are obese. There's never a good time to be overweight, but the earlier it starts, the harder it is to reverse those habits.

A Boy Should Know How to Tie at Tie began by explaining the importance of valuing yourself. If you do think of yourself as worthwhile, then you need to take care of your most valuable possession—your body. And if you value yourself and your body, it all begins with what you put into that body—the food you eat.

Back to My Story

As I sat in my doctor's office with LaNette waiting for the results of the latest exam, I was feeling pretty good about the changes I'd made. After all, for quite a few years, I hadn't eaten red meat, cheese, or pork. I wasn't a vegetarian, but I knew that my diet should help keep my cholesterol levels manageable.

My doctor, a young guy in his midthirties, is the picture of good health. I sometimes kid him that he should make a career out of playing a doctor in a soap opera. He has a great bedside manner, but I could tell something was up as he looked over some results. Then he told me, "Your cholesterol level has gone up to 175. That's too high. I know that you've made some modifications to your lifestyle, and the rest of your results are absolutely fine. We need to do something about this cholesterol level, though. I don't want to take any chances."

LaNette and I looked at each other and exchanged a kind of *Damned right!* expression. We certainly didn't want to take any chances—especially when you think about exactly what those chances are. My doctor said that he was making a call that day to Cedars-Sinai Medical Center, one of Los Angeles's best, for me to undergo further tests. He wanted to be certain that I hadn't sustained any heart damage due to my elevated levels. With the use of a sophisticated scanning machine, he'd be able to determine if any of my arteries had a build up of plaque in them. Fun, right?

"Antwone, from everything I can determine based on my

examination, there doesn't seem to be any blockage, but we need to be absolutely certain. How soon can you make it over there?"

Of course, I immediately had visions of *House* or *Grey's Anatomy* and a team of surgeons standing over my opened chest with wires and tubes all over the place. It was all I could do not to show my anxiety and concern in front of LaNette. But I did what I had to do and I got myself to the medical testing center. I'm happy to say the results were good and I can go on living pretty much as I always have. I'm lucky, but sometimes when we don't take proper care of ourselves, the wake-up call can have a much different outcome.

Invasion of the Memory Monsters

I remembered a phone call I'd received a few months earlier from Kevin Burkley, the brother of a good friend of mine. I had developed a friendship with Fletcher Keith Burkley when we were in the navy together and we remained close over the years. He was a well-read intellectual who was just great to be around. Unfortunately, during that post navy time, Keith had told me that he was diagnosed with diabetes. But his brother was calling with the worst news possible. Keith had been killed in a car accident. They didn't know exactly what happened, but the authorities suspected that he blacked out from diabetic shock while behind the wheel. His car ran onto an embankment and into oncoming traffic where he slammed into an SUV and was killed instantly. Kevin told me the heartbreaking news as he and I took a final walk around Keith's apartment. He told me he could feel the last traces of his brother's presence in the objects in his house.

Before his untimely death, Keith had talked with me about how he wanted to improve his diet and overall heath. He knew that diabetes was something that he needed to be concerned about because a few of his brothers and sisters had developed the disease. None of them were overweight, but it was something that ran in his family. Eventually Keith did develop diabetes and he felt constrained by the disease. He could do most things, but he hated having to be so vigilant about what he ate and when, measuring his blood sugar levels and all that. Because I'm a father now and I'm not a kid myself anymore, losing a friend like Keith made me think about how precious our time here really is. I'd been lucky enough to have made some choices earlier in life about what food I ate and how I cared for myself, but things could have been different. And even with those choices, I was still faced with potential risks.

Start Now

I like eating as much as the next person, and I've had a pretty normal relationship with food throughout my life. I definitely have my weaknesses—chocolate!—but you have to enjoy your indulgences as well as all the stuff that's good for you.

I knew that my body's cholesterol level might simply be a matter of genetics. Funny how some things came with me from my biological parents that I never even thought about. If that were true, there wasn't a thing that I could do about this predisposition. It was the result of a cosmic roll of the dice, and happened to come up with an unlucky number. That doesn't mean that I can just throw my hands up in the air and say, "Well, if that's the hand I've been dealt, then I may as well go all in," and start wolfing down chocolate chip cookies or BLTs.

The first thing I tried to do was educate myself a little bit about the heart. After all, as far as our circulation goes, it's the motor that powers us and makes everything else possible. Recent research done by Dr. Gregg C. Fonarow, a professor of cardiovascular medicine and science at the University of California, Los Angeles, had shown that half the people in cardiac hospital units and 80 percent of those people who had heart attacks had the same cholesterol levels as people who were considered "heart healthy." That led doctors to wonder why it was that so many people, including doctors, thought that cholesterol levels were an indicator of heart disease. Some doctors even believed that it was possible to reverse heart disease, as well as prevent it. Basically, the new research was showing that what some people thought of as a hereditary death sentence didn't have to be one if you took the right steps.

So maybe what I couldn't control, I could at least impact in a positive way. All the good things I'd been doing and the hard work I'd put into exercising had paid off in that my situation was not worse. I had high cholesterol but I was one of those people whose cholesterol level wasn't an indication of heart disease. I was enormously relieved to learn all that. I could do some additional things to lower my cholesterol level, but my heart was essentially as healthy as the rest of me. Even without realizing the consequences that our diets have, I was able to make some good choices. I'm putting all of this on your radar now so that you can think about it.

A Fortunate Choice

I stopped eating red meat when I was in the navy. It wasn't because of any moral issues I had about the treatment of animals. Living with the Picketts had already made me squeamish about eating meat. They were old-school southerners and even though we lived in Cleveland, we had a steady diet of game—rabbits, squirrel, the occasional deer—and there was something about seeing the whole animal being butchered that grossed me out. Sometimes they would have a pig roast, and I can still see the hollowed out animal, sliced in half but with its head intact, roasting on a spit. I sometimes feel that because we are so far removed from the living animal and the butchering process that it's easy for us to forget about where the meat we eat comes from. As a result of the Picketts' habits, meat wasn't a big part of my life. Neither was eating, frankly. Meal time at the Picketts' a wasn't a social occasion at all. Instead, everyone sat in their chairs and gnawed away at whatever was put in front of them. Except for the sound of their grunting and their lips smacking, mealtime was purposeful and boring. No one made any real attempt at human connection. Whatever your situation, mealtime should be enjoyed as a social opportunity as well as a time to eat good, healthful food. At home, that means finding out around the dinner table how everyone's day went. For work, there's a book called *Never Eat Alone* by Keith Ferrazzi that suggests lunch hour as a great chance to build relationships and further your career.

In the navy, I made my decision. When you consider that a typical cruise lasts nine months and you are far away from any land for much of it, the only choice is to freeze the supplies. Because the navy was feeding hundreds and hundreds of men onboard ship, that frozen food wasn't always as tasty as I would have liked. Fresh fruits and vegetables were scarce. I didn't like the taste of frozen meat, and once I stopped eating it, I actually started feeling less sluggish and generally better. And when I felt better physically, I was able to accomplish more and stay on top of my game. Funny how things work that way.

What It Means to Eat Healthfully

Let's get started to make sure you are fueling your body with the right kind of stuff. Nearly every dietician and fitness expert recommends that you keep a food diary. Before you can evaluate the quality of your diet, you need to have a clear idea of what it is, right? Here's a simple food diary chart that you can fill in.

TIME	FOOD ITEM	QUANTITY	CALORIE CONTENT
Morning			
Afternoon			
Evening			

You'll need more lines than what I've shown here, but you get the idea. Quantity and calorie content might be more difficult for you to keep track of, but if you read the label on some of the foods you eat, you'll be able to get the weight and calories. Since that's not always possible, there are many online sources that give you a lot of information about the kinds of foods we typically eat, including calorie counts. I use the online resource www.nutritiondata.com. It is a great site and in addition to telling you the number of total calories, it reproduces the label found on the packaging and gives you a breakdown of some of the pluses and minuses of what you're eating. For examples, if you ate a Whopper from Burger King, you could find all the nutritional data on that item by entering "Whopper" in the search field at the top of the home page. You'd find out that a Whopper with no cheese weighs in at 291 grams (more than ten ounces), it has 37 grams of fat in it (almost an ounce and a half—57 percent of your daily recommended intake of fat), and a whole lot more including a quick list of what's good and what's bad for you. For a Whopper, there's some good because it is high in some vitamins, but bad as well because it contains trans fats—the worst kind of fat you can consume. *Eat This, Not That* by David Zinczenko is also a good resource for this kind of information and books with calorie information are readily available in your bookstore or library.

How Much Should You Consume?

So once you track your intake for a day, you can compare the number of calories you consumed to the recommended number of calories for a person your age and gender. According to the U.S. Department of Agriculture, here's what the general recommendations are:

TEENAGERS	CALORIES
Boys: 11–14 yrs	2,220
Girls: 11–14 yrs	1,845

TEENAGERS	CALORIES
Boys: 15–18 yrs	2,755
Girls: 15–18 yrs	2,110

ADULTS	CALORIES
Men: 19–50 yrs	2,550
Women: 19–50 yrs	1,940

These are rough guidelines, and depending upon how active you are (more on this in a moment), you should adjust your caloric intake. There is a lot of information about the proper caloric intake, and Web sites like the Mayo Clinic's can be excellent resources. But if you don't have the wherewithal to dive too deep into analyzing what you eat, and the thought of crunching all those numbers turns you off, there are a few basics that you should always keep in mind. Fresh foods will, for the most part, be better for you than processed foods. Fruits, vegetables, and lean meats are excellent sources of nutrition. Generally, when you are in the supermarket, it's the food you find on the outer track of the store, in refrigerated bins, that's better. Stay away from the stuff in the middle of the store as much as you can. And in addition to calories, keep an eye on the salt in the premade foods you buy. Most Americans have too much salt in their diets and this is unhealthy over the long run. The flip side of that is to stay well-hydrated and water is the best way to do that. Sweetened drinks like sodas or even sports drinks are loaded with stuff such as high fructose corn syrup, which should be avoided as much as possible.

The Balanced Diet

If you are looking for some guidelines about how much of each kind of food to eat, here are some guidelines for the three major kinds of macronutrients. (Macronutrients are the three classes of chemical compounds we consume in the greatest quantity and provide us with energy.) The general consensus is 50 to 60 percent of your daily calorie intake should come from carbohydrates, 30 percent from protein; and 10 to 20 percent from fats. Good proteins include lean beef and pork, white-meat poultry such as turkey breast, and eggs, beans, and tofu. Yes, after years of getting a bad rap, eggs are a great source of protein as well as certain minerals. Good carbohydrates can be found in whole-grain breads and cereals, oatmeal, fruits, and vegetables. The less refined white bread in your diet, the better. Lastly, not all fats are created equal. I mentioned trans fats—these are the worst. They are generally found in packaged, processed food and you should keep an eye out for them on the nutrition label. What you really want are the healthy fats found in fish, nuts, and sources like avocados or olive oil. Lean meat and milk are also good sources, but remember, everything in moderation.

You certainly don't need to become a vegetarian like me or make radical changes in your eating habits, so be aware of what you're eating and make the necessary changes.

Get Cooking

Let's face it. There's a tradition among women to keep each other company in the kitchen. Frequently, for girls this means keeping mom or an aunt company while they cook, socializing and passing on family recipes. That's great for us guys because we can hang out in the living room watching football. It's great until you need to cook for yourself and you can't tell a whisk from a spatula. When it comes to the basics of health, avoiding fast-food joints and having control of how much stuff such as salt goes into your food are big steps to a healthy diet. But, hey, cooking isn't manly, right? Wrong. I have to point out that some of the great chefs today—guys like Bobby Flay and Mario Batali—appear to be some of the coolest guys around. So I'm going to include a couple of basic recipes here that are a great fallback with some whole ingredients. One of them uses canned ingredients to show that a mixture of canned and fresh can be fast, convenient, and economical.

Turkey Cassoulet

Serves 2 to 4

Here's a simple recipe that combines turkey and beans, both a great source of protein. This serves plenty, so it's a good dish to make at the beginning of the week and refrigerate for future meals. Or if you're hanging out with your friends, it will feed a crowd inexpensively.

1 pound spicy turkey sausage, cut into ½-inch pieces
1 cup uncooked orzo pasta
2 teaspoons minced garlic
One 14½-ounce can salt-free stewed tomatoes, undrained
1½ cups water
1 teaspoon dried thyme leaves
1 teaspoon table salt
½ teaspoon ground black pepper
One 16- to 19-ounce can white kidney beans or great Northern beans, drained
    and rinsed
One 15-ounce can mixed vegetables, drained

In a large saucepan with a lid, cook the sausage over medium heat for 10 to 12 minutes until no pink remains. Add the orzo and garlic and stir constantly for 5 to 7 minutes, or until the orzo begins to brown. Add the remaining ingredients; stir gently, cover, and cook for 20 to 25 minutes, until the orzo is al dente, stirring occasionally. Serve with a crisp green salad.

A Chicken Dinner

Having a woman over for a dinner that you prepared yourself lets her know that you value her. Cooking a dinner that is both delicious and healthful increases that value. Many people love fried chicken, and using your mother's or your grandmother's recipe to create a crispy and delicious main course might seem like the way to go. What you have to remember is that previous generations didn't have the resources and knowledge available to them that you have. Fried chicken is delicious, but fried foods contain too much fat. Fast-food chicken is a good example of a great idea gone bad. By itself, chicken is not a high-fat food. Most of the fat content results from how it's prepared. For example, one-half a chicken breast boned and skinned only has 26 grams of fat. That same amount of chicken with the skin and bones and fried has 100 grams of fat—four times as much.

Of course, fried chicken is delicious and boiled chicken (the method that would add the least amount of fat to the cooking process) isn't nearly as good. The following recipe will help you get all the flavor of fried chicken without all the added fat. You can even include the skin to give it that crispy texture that makes fried chicken a delight to all your senses. Even better, baking a chicken doesn't require as much of your attention and cleanup!

Crisp Baked Chicken

Serves 2 to 4

2 to 4 split chicken breasts, bone in
¼ cup all purpose flour
1 teaspoon table salt (optional)
1 teaspoon fresh ground black pepper
herbs and spices to taste
2 egg whites
⅓ cup skim or 2% milk
1 teaspoon pepper sauce (optional)
1¼ cups bread crumbs

Cover a baking sheet with waxed paper and set aside. Remove the skin and any fat you see on the chicken breast. (You can leave the skin on, but the fat content will be higher!) In a large bowl combine the flour, salt, black pepper, and any other herbs and spices you might like (thyme, oregano, rosemary). Combine in a large bowl and beat with a fork the egg whites and milk. If you want spicy chicken, you can add 1 teaspoon hot pepper sauce to the mix. Sprinkle the bread crumbs onto another sheet of wax paper (about a 1-foot section will do). Take each chicken breast and place it meaty-side down in the flour mixture; dip it into the milk mixture; then roll it in the bread crumbs. At each dunking, make sure that you have coated the chicken completely and evenly. After each piece is coated with bread crumbs, place it on a piece of plastic wrap. Once all the pieces are coated, wrap them up and place in the refrigerator for an hour. Preheat the oven to 350°F. Place the chicken pieces on the baking sheet. If you have a small wire rack you can place that on the sheet and place the chicken on top of the rack. That will allow the underside of the pieces to get crispy as well. Bake until the juices run clear when you pierce the chicken with a fork. This should take about 45 to 55 minutes.

Fat Content: 13 grams

Baked Sweet Potato

Serves 1

Wrap a sweet potato in a piece of aluminum foil and place it in the oven along with the chicken. For a variation, slice the potato in half, drizzle olive oil on both inside halves, and sprinkle with salt and pepper. Fit the pieces back together and wrap in foil as above. If you want sweeter sweet potatoes, sprinkle some cinnamon on them instead of the salt and pepper. Believe it or not, sweet potatoes have less starch (and therefore less sugar and fewer calories) than white potatoes. You can also substitute butter for the olive oil, but that will increase the saturated (bad) fat content. One pat (teaspoon) of butter has fewer overall fat calories than a teaspoon of olive oil (36 vs. 40) but the saturated fat content of butter is 13 percent compared to olive oil's 3 percent. Remember, it's not just how much fat, but what kind of fat. Unsaturated is better than saturated!

Fat content: 2 grams for the potato and 40 grams per teaspoon of olive oil

Blanched Green Beans

Makes 4 ½ cup servings

Fresh is always better than canned, so I recommend that you buy fresh beans and cook by either blanching or steaming instead of just reheating a can of beans (which has way too much salt).

Rinse 1 pound of beans and cut off the end where the stem is. In a shallow frying pan, place enough water to fill the pan halfway. Add a pinch of salt to the water—that will keep the beans a nice bright green. Bring the water to a boil over high heat. When the water is boiling, place the beans in the pan. Reduce the heat to a simmer and cover. Depending upon how crisp you like your vegetables, the cooking time will vary from about 5 minutes to 15 minutes. When they are at the desired crispness, remove the beans from the pain and drain off the excess water. You can season them with salt and pepper and olive oil or squeeze fresh lemon juice on them.

The fresh flavors of the beans and potato will be a nice complement to the chicken. Also, the colors of the items will look really good on the plate—remember that even in cooking, appearances matter.

Fat content: 40 grams per teaspoon of olive oil

Get a Move On

In addition to eating well, the truth is that you can't be truly healthy without incorporating exercise into your daily routine. (Remember that routine I asked you to think about? How much of your day was spent doing active things like playing sports, running, or even just walking?) Along with consuming too many calories on average, most of us just aren't burning enough calories by being active. The Centers for Disease Control and Prevention has issued new guidelines for the amount of exercise children, adults, and older adults should engage in. This isn't so much about weight loss as it is about overall fitness and, most important, disease prevention. The CDC's guidelines break exercise down into three categories: aerobic, muscle-strengthening, and bone-strengthening activities. Aerobic refers to your heart and lungs (your cardiovascular system) and the CDC recommends that young people engage in at least sixty minutes a day of activities that get you moving. They define these everyday activities as moderately aerobic—walking, for example. They also suggest that kids engage in vigorous aerobic activity, such as running, three times a week as a part of that hour a day. Muscle-strengthening exercise such as lifting weights, sit-ups, and push-ups should be performed three times a week and also count toward that sixty-minute-a-day total. Bone-strengthening exercises such as running and jumping rope are also recommended three times a week. How much of this kind of exercise do you get in a week?

To understand some of these issues better, I spoke with Lindsay Brin, a fitness guru and former NFL cheerleader. (Hey, I had to have *some* fun writing this book, right?) She's served as a trainer for thousands of clients, and we spoke about nutrition and fitness. She said, "I know that sixty minutes a day sounds like a lot. I know how busy kids are and how scheduled their lives are with various activities. If those activities are sports related, especially something like soccer, then they're getting their sixty minutes in pretty easily."

She went on to explain the benefits of interval training as one of the most important concepts in exercise and fitness. "Basically, interval training means alternating periods of low-, medium-, and high-intensity effort while you are exercising. You have to do that because our bodies are amazingly adaptable. They adjust to whatever effort you ask of them. If you walk three miles a day every day at the same pace, you won't be getting the same benefit after a few weeks as you did at the beginning. You reach a plateau. Besides, if you do interval training, you can maximize the results from a shorter workout."

Her suggested walking/running plan would go something like this: Warm up by walking at a moderate pace for ten minutes. How do you know what's moderate? If you are walking with someone else, you should be able to speak in a normal tone without your breathing being labored. After that warm-up period, do two to three minutes of faster walking, jogging, or running. You should feel your heart and breathing rates going up. It should be much harder to maintain a conversation. After those two minutes are up, slow down to your moderate pace for two minutes. Repeat the pattern for at least ten minutes and then cool down with a moderate walk for at least two minutes.

Jeff Galloway, who has trained thousands of people to run marathons, recommends the same pattern of walking and running. You may not have a goal of covering twenty-six miles, but if you follow this interval training plan, you're on your way to being able to do just that. If you are interested in a challenge like completing a running race—whether it is a 5K, 10K, half marathon, or full marathon—you can find great tips on how to meet your goal at www .jeffgalloway.com. Whether you're someone who has never run or you've done some training like what I just suggested, there are programs available for you to follow.

Moderation

Anything in moderation is a good rule of thumb, but many of us never learn, except the hard way, what that concept really means. It isn't like we're all born knowing what's enough and what's too much, whether we're talking about food, alcohol, or watching television.

I've been fortunate to find those boundaries on my own, but not everybody does or can. If one enjoys better circumstances than I did as a young man, that's even more of a reason to exercise good judgment and not put yourself or your health at risk.

Men and Alcohol

Things like heart health and obesity are long-term risks for boys and men. But one of the most immediate risks we face as young men is alcoholism. From drinking and driving to stupid decisions to the simple overconsumption of alcohol, many of us face peer pressure from an early age. It is illegal to consume alcohol under the age of twenty-one in the United States, and one of the best decisions you can make is to pass on alcohol until you are an adult. Even then, of course, the risks continue. I was fortunate in that I never really liked alcohol the few times I tried it growing up. I didn't like the taste and I didn't like the way it made me feel like I was no longer in control. Perhaps I felt that way the most when I was homeless and I had to have my senses completely together twenty-four hours a day. Of course, I was in the navy and most of us did a certain amount of drinking in the social context of celebrating shore leave and occasions like that.

I remember one night in Hong Kong shortly after I was on my first cruise. One of the senior chiefs and a lieutenant commander bought me a drink. I'd gone along on shore leave to hang out with everyone and to feel like a part of the group. Senior Chief Lawrence kind of assumed the role of my big brother. Knowing a bit of my history, I don't think he wanted me to be out there with my peers unprotected. Because I was with him and the lieutenant commander, I felt safe drinking so I had just a little bit.

I was one of the few sailors who was like that. Most of the rest of the guys drank to get drunk and didn't seem to enjoy themselves until they were. In a way, drinking until intoxicated while in the navy was a safe way to do it (though the navy does not approve of underage drinking or drunken sailors) because we were usually surrounded by fellow shipmates, and we knew to watch out for one another. I don't remember any serious incidents that occurred with guys drinking while on liberty or while stationed on a base. It seemed that guys got in trouble when they were away from the disciplined environment of the service. I heard the story of a fellow serviceman with whom I served on the USS *Robert E. Perry*. He was killed in a motorcycle accident while under the influence of alcohol. We all heard about a marine who died of alcohol poisoning while in the Philippines. And it seems as if no matter how hard colleges try to crack down on hazing, you hear a story like that every fall. What a terrible and needless way to die.

Alcohol and Control

I know that for a lot of young people, drinking is a way to feel powerful and in control. Because alcohol has an effect on our inhibitions and loosens them up, we often say and do things that we wouldn't without it. In the navy we were mostly a bunch of young guys who went out together, and if there was one thing that really united us all, it was that we were a walking bundle of insecurity. Sure, our military duties required us to move tons of equipment worth millions of dollars, but those skills didn't really help us when it came to simple socializing. Being in a foreign land was exciting and scary. The fact that we went out in groups and tended to go to bars and clubs where U.S. military men were regulars is evidence of that insecurity. Drinking gave us all a false sense of security. That was just something I couldn't really tolerate on a regular basis—and neither should you.

It's ironic that in order to feel powerful and in control, young people choose to drink something that makes them less powerful and in less control. I'm not completely opposed to drinking, and I think that it's okay for young men to enjoy a beer at a ballgame (when they are of legal age, of course). I just wish that everyone could do it in a safe and controlled environment. I believe that because there wasn't any alcohol in the house I grew up in, because I wasn't exposed to it, I wasn't as fascinated by it as many of my peers. I'm going to follow those same practices in my own house with my kids.

Drugs

The first time someone offered me marijuana, it was easy for me to refuse. My friend Jessie and I were both about eleven years old. Jessie was one of my longtime childhood friends. We were just strutting along the streets of our neighborhood when he reached into his pocket and pulled out a joint. He said, "Hey, man, you want to smoke this with me?"

I said, "I don't smoke."

And he said, "Well, this will make us feel good. We can smoke this, and then we can have more fun. We can go over here and stand in front of the record store. And the music will sound better."

I thought about that for a second as we continued to walk along. How could a drug make music sound better? I also thought of my teacher Mrs. Profit and all the things she told me about drugs and the negative things that could happen to me if I started doing them. So I said to Jessie, "Well, I don't want to take any drugs. I don't want to smoke anything."

He screwed his face up in disgust and said, "Aww, man! What is wrong with you?" He sped up and left me trailing in his wake.

When I'd ask guys like Jessie what it was like to be high they'd say something like, "Well, man, I feel good. I feel like I could do anything." Jessie in particular would tell me that he felt like he was a better dancer when under the influence. He'd stand in front of that record store and sing. We'd all be standing there, and he would spin around on his heels and dance. But he was falling all over the place, looking like a fool. People were laughing at him, and he was so high that he took that as a compliment, mistaking their response as some sort of approval.

As a child, I lived in constant fear that I would give the Picketts an excuse to get rid of me, to "send me back," as Mizz Pickett constantly threatened. And while I did act out on certain occasions, I generally respected the rules and toed the line. On the other hand, Jessie lived with his mother. I'm sure she never threatened to send him away. Whatever experimenting we did, I didn't have the luxury of crossing certain lines. And just because you have the luxury of crossing those lines, doesn't mean that you're entitled to. When I faced peer pressure about drinking, smoking, or taking drugs, I might have been given a hard time initially, but eventually people accepted that I didn't do those things.

Healthy, Wealthy, and Wise

You can invent and reinvent yourself countless times. I was able to rise from being born in a prison to awards shows with the biggest celebrities in Hollywood to having lunch in the White House apartment of the president of the United States. I have a wife and two children where I had never had a real family before. And I was lucky enough to have made a few decisions along the way that kept my body from suffering even worse than my mind had. Everything is possible in the world, but you will want your body to be in great shape so that it can take you places.

We live in a world of competing influences and challenges. On the one hand, many of us have little time left over from work or school, and exercising and eating right feel more like luxuries than facts of life. We drive to and from the movie theater or the mall. Big food companies sell us food with health benefits that don't hold up. On the other hand, there is more good information than ever available on how to treat your body well and make the right kind of choices. These are decisions you can make in your teens and twenties from which you will reap the benefits for years to come. I've given you just a few of the basics when it comes to nutrition, exercise, and healthy living. A boy should be curious about these things and I hope that this has fed your hunger for more knowledge on the subject. Now go find those soccer cleats you rediscovered after cleaning your room following chapter eight and go find a pick-up game in the park.

CHAPTER TEN

DEVELOP YOUR SPIRITUAL SIDE

After the navy and three years as a corrections officer at a federal correctional institution called Terminal Island, I was a security officer on the lot of Sony Studios when I decided to set out and find whatever family I might have left in the world. Through some amateur sleuthing and some great good fortune, I was ultimately reunited with and embraced by my father's family years after his death. I found I had aunts, uncles, and countless cousins. These were people who were nearby as I struggled in my childhood, and yet they were strangers until now.

I also met my mother, Eva Mae Fisher. It was a painful reunion for both of us. But it allowed me to understand the circumstances that beset a woman who had given me up to the state. It allowed me some peace and understanding that had escaped me all those years.

Surviving the streets, finding my family, and then starting a family of my own surely meant someone or something had smiled down on me at my darkest moments. But the question of religion has haunted me my whole life. The Reverand Pickett was a God-fearing Christian, "fear" being the operative word. But his true values flew in the face of the Christianity he preached—he was a man who allowed cruelty to children to exist on a daily basis under his own roof without raising a finger. And as I related earlier, one of my first successful acts of defiance, of breaking free from the Picketts' abuse, was to refuse to go to church one day. In fact, when I returned to Cleveland and was reunited with the Elkinses and the Fishers, I refused to pursue any kind of reunion with the Picketts. My feelings about religion are clouded by my experiences, but that doesn't mean I didn't spend my life searching for the kind of meaning and peace that many people, including perhaps you, find in religion.

Even with all those painful memories, I don't level a sweeping accusation against those who do believe, who do pray, who do attend church regularly. I admire those people who live out their faith in action, and I hold no grudge nor cast any stones towards those who either practice no religion or who fail to heed the tenets of their professed faith. I am not about to elevate myself to the level of God and suppose that I am capable of making those kinds of judgments.

An Important Distinction

To make sense of things, I've come to understand a difference between what we call religion and spirituality. In my mind, and as I live it, religion is the belief in a formal set of teachings inspired by God but put in place by man. Spirituality is a fundamental belief that along with our physical bodies, we also exist on a different energy plane. As much as we are composed of a corporal self made of flesh and bone, we are spirit. Religion and spirituality coexist and share one elemental similarity: they are both rooted in faith. Just as I can't find absolute physical evidence to prove, for example, that Zacheus was a man of small stature and great wealth who lived in Jericho and climbed a tree so that he could see Jesus, I can't find absolute physical evidence to prove that a human's spiritual energy outlives the physical body. Something inside me tells me that our spirits will go on, and that deep sense of knowing provides me with a lot of comfort and hope, in the same way those who believe in the Bible and God's active presence also find hope in their deep sense of knowing. Every religion, every spiritual practice that I know of, share one thing in common. It is a fundamental principle that underlies all "faiths": there is more to us than our physical bodies, and the time we spend here walking this earth is but a brief moment in our existence.

Hope is a wonderful thing. From wherever it springs, we should be glad that we are near its source and can drink from it.

A History Lesson

Historically, as a people, we African Americans looked to God for deliverance from the hands of our oppressors. As hard as it may be for you to believe, my foster father (who was in his fifties when I was living with him) was old enough back in the 1960s and '70s to have memories of relatives who had lived as slaves. Here we all are, in the second decade of the twenty-first century, and I can make that statement. I sometimes think my foster father's preaching style was deeply influenced by those relatives. He was one of those fiery preachers who knew that fear was a powerful motivator. I remember him telling the story of Samson killing the Philistines with the jawbone of an ass. He was up in front of the congregation, and he rose up to his full height, puffed out his chest, and the enormous whites of his eyes stood out in stark contrast to his face. In front of me, he transformed himself from the gray-haired man who moved around the house without uttering a word into a fearsome warrior. He brought his hands down on the lectern time and time and again, the thudding blows echoing throughout the hall where we'd gathered. I sat there in shock and horror, my heart beating faster at the thought of this man Samson beating and beating on these other men until they were a bloody, pulpy mess. In my mind, celebrating that heroic victory seemed to be about the most un-Christian thing a person could do. Why was my foster father taking such joy in recounting that story?

As I got older, I realized that he hadn't lived in slavery himself, but he had heard those stories of his people held in bondage. For that reason, the stories from the Bible of the Israelites held in slavery seemed to really resonate with him. He seemed to dwell on those stories of captivity and enslavement, and the message he seemed to be preaching was that if we weren't careful, if we weren't good, if we didn't toe the line, we could end up right back there in that same predicament as our ancestors and long before them, the Israelites. He peppered his lessons with stories of the vengeful, wrathful God of the Old Testament, and for a long time, I associated the word "smote" with God. Today, I know that my youthful associations of God and smiting are way off base, but still that element of fear in my foster father's preaching holds a note of truth.

Contrast that fear with the hope that most people associate with God. I don't know what it was that possessed him to place the emphasis on one and not the other. I do know that the slaves found in their belief in a God the kind of hope that allowed them to endure.

Listening to the Flip Side

Much of my thinking has been shaped by the fact that I had a twentieth-century foster father who seemed to have a nineteenth-century mind-set. I realize that many of the people who regularly attend church and put their faith in God share the same ideas I do regarding spirituality. What troubles me though is that I sometimes think that as a people—and I see this especially in a lot of young people—we don't believe in ourselves, and we don't have as much faith in our own capabilities as we should. One of the reasons why we as a people and I as an individual have been able to overcome so much is because we ultimately came to believe in our own power to make great changes in our circumstances. In my case, belief in self and belief in my self as spirit, as something that transcended a particular place or point in time, moved mountains.

What I'm suggesting isn't a drastic departure from what preachers have been saying for a long time. What I've experienced is a gradual shift in perspective based on my experiences. When you're a young person, formal religious training is deeply influential. You hear what your elders in the church, in your family, in your community, tell you. You respect those people—and you should, and you should listen to what they say—but you have little of your own experience in life against which to test those ideas. Faith, as I've said, is a wonderful thing. Faith based on fear, whether it's the fear of a wrathful vengeful version of God, fear of questioning authority, or fear of the unknown, is not a good thing.

I had to put to the test what I'd been taught. If I had simply accepted my experience as a young person, I might easily have assumed that all religious people were hypocrites. They preached one thing on Sunday and acted in a far different way the rest of the week. Fortunately, I didn't accept that. I learned that the family who raised me and instructed me in the ways of God was deeply flawed. It was them, and not God, whose ways were bent. Just as I couldn't dismiss everything I had been taught in church because of how they acted, I also couldn't accept what I witnessed as the only truth, either. I had to go out in the world. The result of that choice is my sense of spirituality.

My Spiritual Path

I didn't always believe what I do today. I began with a firm foundation in Christianity. But once I left Reverend Pickett's house and was on my own, I can't say that my faith wavered, but my desire to be a part of a formal church ended. When I was homeless, I was spiritually homeless as well. When your life revolves around making certain that your physical body is safe, security becomes your primary and nearly exclusive concern. That's also one of the reasons I devoted a fair amount of *A Boy Should Know How to Tie a Tie* to issues relating to our bodies and appearance. From a healthy and secure body, we can set out to explore less tangible ideas. I've never been the type of person who turned to God as the source of either my distress or my pleasure. When I was homeless or when I was in the worst of places with the Picketts, I never blamed God for my condition. It wasn't that I didn't believe in the power of prayer; it was more that I felt God had other concerns. I wasn't searching for God or a spiritual answer because I believed that the spirit was inside me and that it would eventually enable me to realize all my dreams.

My life still revolved around Christian concepts up until the time I entered the navy. It was at that point, as I began to travel the world and encounter people with different beliefs, that I understood there were other ways to see the world, ways much different from the tiny world of Cleveland, Ohio. In Japan, I befriended a man by the name of Yuu Fukushima. He had attended college in the United States, so he was a fairly fluent in English. One spring, as Easter approached, a lot of us were excited about the coming holiday.

Yuu-san and I were talking and we discussed my plans for Easter. He knew about the Western tradition of Easter baskets and the Easter bunny and all that. I expected him to find that odd. I commented on this, but to my surprise he said, "I have a harder time believing that a man can be executed and then three days later live again." I can still remember sitting there and feeling my jaw drop and my mouth hang open. I had to blink a few times before I could respond. "Yuu-san, what do you mean? How can you not believe in Jesus and his resurrection?"

He went on to explain that he wasn't raised in the Christian tradition. "I'm a Buddhist," he said, as if that would explain everything to me. I'd been in Japan for a while and I knew a little bit about the culture. It wasn't until then that I realized that I didn't see a lot of churches or other "traditional" places of worship. Yuu-san explained that most Japanese didn't actively participate in religion the way Westerners do. He said that most Japanese were either Buddhists like himself or followers of Shintoism. Jesus didn't figure in either of those two traditions, so when he learned about Jesus Christ, it sounded to him more like a story than a fundamental basis for a religion. After that discussion, I was curious about Eastern religion mostly from a cultural perspective. I didn't delve deeply into ancient texts, but my eyes were opened to the world in a new way.

Following my new awareness, I started to spot Buddhist temples or Shinto shrines where I'd never noticed them before. In my travels around Japan, I went to visit some of them, like Tokyo's Meiji shrine and Kyoto's Heian shrine. I admired them as much for their architectural beauty—I especially liked the torii gates, shaped like Japanese characters—as I did their religious significance. As my tours of duty took me to other parts of the world, I came to realize that in many places Christians were a minority and followers of Islam the majority. I can't say that I was like Saint Paul on the road from Damascus and was knocked from my horse and later had the scales removed from my eyes to alleviate my blindness. I was more aware that religion and matters of faith were much more diverse than I had originally thought or experienced.

This real-world education was good for me. I became much

more open-minded and aware that my world was very, very small in comparison to the rest of the world. I wasn't really in a quest to find a new set of beliefs to replace those I had in place, but I was expanding my understanding.

My Education Continues

My education continued after the navy as well. Now that I have children and they attend a Catholic school, I've been confronted with some of these questions again. My older daughter Indigo seems to really take her religious instruction in Catholicism to heart. She says her nightly prayers, kneeling beside her bed. There are times when I am tempted to step in and say something about the nature of her prayers, especially when they start more like a wish-list than a statement of appreciation.

I was reading Ray Charles's autobiography, *Brother Ray*, and I came across a passage in which he revealed his thoughts on prayer. He stated that he recited the Lord's Prayer every night before going to sleep. He sometimes said other prayers, but as he put it, "only after I've done all I could on my own." I liked that idea and it dovetailed with my sense of belief in the power of self. Charles went on to say, "As long as I can stand it, God, I'll keep on keeping on. I say: When I can do a little bit more on my own, Lord, I'll do it. I say: If I have strength left in me, then I'll use it."

The tension between relying on self and relying on God is one that I saw as a black and white issue as a younger man. I believed that relying on God meant that I was giving up faith in myself and vice versa.

Today, I can see that was a pretty immature attitude for me to take. In previous chapters, I've written about how I came to value myself. I'm not sure where that sense of my own value came from, but when I consider it now, I realize that I must have had a sense of my God-endowed value even during my darkest days when everything told me that I was worthless. That spiritual part of me was something I'd been entrusted with and needed to take care of. I must have understood, though I certainly couldn't have articulated it, that there was some spirit, some energy inside of me that would eventually enable me to rise above the rough circumstances of my life and to prosper.

That point was driven home for me at a recent appearance I made in New York. I was asked to speak at a conference there. After my presentation, there was the usual meet-and-greet gathering. A woman came up to me and told me how remarkable my story of personal transformation was. I thanked her, and then she said, "You know, God was with you the whole time." I thanked her again, and it was only on the plane ride back that I took the time to fully consider what she had said. God has been with me my whole life. In realizing that, I also understood why it was that I didn't ever feel the need to go looking for God or an established religion whose teachings I should follow. I understood why it was that I didn't need to go find God in a building. That spirit is in me. Where I need to go is inside myself to get in touch with the power.

A Missing Piece

All that said, I do miss one part of being a part of an organized religion: the sense of community that comes with it. The sense of belonging that I so desired as a young man was something that I might have found if I'd been able to attend a church other than the Picketts'. Churches are the centers of a thriving social network. As a young person, your sense of belonging and a desire to fit in is likely to be greater than it is for someone of my age. As I've said before, aligning yourself with the right group, the right influences are important, and I can think of no better place than a church. Many churches are quite progressive and offer programs where you help the local community. Churches also sponsor trips abroad where you too can expand your horizons.

It is your duty as a young person to explore as many avenues as possible, to experience as much as you possibly can, and to learn what your strengths and weaknesses are. You may be surprised to find that you have an inner calling that manifests itself in a more outward display of your faith. By giving hope to others, we find hope for ourselves. There is an alienating aspect to all of the technology that is increasingly important in our lives. Facebook, Twitter, and so on. A church community is a real way to maintain face-to-face contact with people and keep yourself grounded in the world. Oddly enough, it was my time at reform school that also opened up a side of spirituality in my life. That was one of the first times I found myself outside of the city in a more natural setting. For the first time, I experienced a certain peace in nature that I think is tremendously important in our lives. Perhaps it's the flip side of maintaining strong ties to a community. It's appreciating the wind through the leaves and the changing sky. It's understanding the beauty of the natural world and searching for our harmony with that world.

The Spirit Moves You

Whatever decisions you ultimately make in your life, religion contains a set of principles from which you can learn. Pay attention to the lessons, even if they seem to come in endless Sunday sermons. As you grow older, you will develop an understanding of your own religious beliefs. The ties to this community can serve you well your whole life, so be respectful of the church and don't be afraid to participate. But don't let your beliefs keep you from changing the world and righting its wrongs where you see them. We need to believe always in the power of the individual to make good acts no matter the motivation.

A BOY SHOULD KNOW
HOW TO LIVE A GOOD LIFE

I recently learned that De'Angelo Wilson, one of the actors who was in the movie *Antwone Fisher*, hanged himself. He was found suspended by a rope in a tree behind a business on Wilshire Boulevard in the heart of Los Angeles. He'd climbed a tree behind the building and threw a noose around its limb. His body wasn't discovered until early the next afternoon. How awful that sight must have been. Years earlier, Denzel Washington discovered De'Angelo while we were filming *Antwone Fisher* in Cleveland and cast him in the role of my childhood friend Jessie. His passing made the news briefly, then the story soon faded into the background, replaced by other bad news. I hated hearing that about De'Angelo. I liked him and I feel he was a genuinely good person. He was the life of the party at some of my backyard get-togethers. I did not know that he had fallen on hard times and was homeless at the time of his death. There just aren't that many acting roles for guys with his looks, acting style, and somewhat limited acting experience. To add to the tragedy, he died at the age of twenty-nine.

He once told LaNette and me about some of the demons from his past that haunted him. We really felt for him but didn't realize the depths of his despair. He felt that acting would be the vehicle that would lead him to a new place. For him, acting was a form of catharsis, a way to express through his craft the emotions that roiled around inside of him. A lot of the young men and women who arrive in Hollywood looking for their big break are vulnerable in one way or another. It can be an incredibly tough town, with just a few openings for success and a lot of opportunities to be turned down. You have to be resilient enough to face all kinds of rejection and willing to do whatever it takes to legally support yourself while you wait for your big break. De'Angelo's story is heartbreaking and dramatic, but there are many similar stories from different parts of the world.

Having met De'Angelo while filming my life story, and with his having portrayed one of the people in my life, I was somehow even more disturbed to see him meet this end. It was again a kind of visceral reminder of the direction my life might have taken had I not persevered or had I lost that kernel of hope deep inside me. No matter what the state of Ohio valued me at, I valued myself and that value has only increased over time.

Having my family with me in good times and bad and knowing that they count on me to be here for them, as I do them, is a wonderful feeling. I am connected to the world in ways that I had always hoped to be. I didn't have a father around to teach me many of the lessons that I've shared with you. I hope that you've benefited from my experiences and insights, just as I hope that you have the loving support of your parents to guide you. I want you to know that along with them and with me, you will encounter many people who are willing to lend you the benefit of their wisdom and experience. But sometimes, it is also up to you to seek them out.

I've been exposed to and experienced some of human beings' worst impulses—I was placed in the foster care system with people who cared very little about me; I've stood on the deck of a navy vessel as we fired missiles across the Gulf of Oman at targets miles away; I've worked in a prison on the aptly named Terminal Island where guards were outnumbered by prisoners 150 to 1, where murderers like the man we all referred to as Black Cloud lived trapped in a mind broken and bent in ways I can't even begin to understand—and yet, I've made it to this place in my life where I hope to be an example for others. There will be people and other forces at work in your life telling you that you are either without value or of low value. You can't let those things overwhelm you. You can ignore those voices and focus on the people who would help you. Value yourself and those negative opinions will matter little as you find your way to success.

I've already mentioned that I heard a tiny little voice amid all the shouting and confusion and negative voices telling me that I was no good. That tiny little voice told me that I was worth something, that I had value, that my life was worth living. In time, that voice was joined by others in a chorus of affirmation letting me know that I mattered.

I hope that my voice and my advice have added to an already existing choir of voices you hear. If you don't hear other people singing your praises, I'm the first of the background singers, and I'm glad to be here for you. Know this: the songs have to start with you. It is your voice out front, loud and strong, that will get others to join in. If those first sounds are a request for help, that's okay. In time, and with help, those words will change from requests for help to statements of your ability and your worth.

How you present yourself outwardly to the world is a reflection of how you feel about yourself inwardly. When you create a vision for yourself and develop a plan for how to realize it, you take control of your life. It took me many years to put all the pieces together, but here I am, offering you the benefit of some of my experience. Take what works for you, discard the rest—better yet, keep it safely and neatly tucked away somewhere so that you can easily access it if the need arises—and pass it on to the next person who may need it.

Yes, there are some bad things in this world, but you can offset that by finding the beautiful things as well, whether that's picking up a musical instrument and playing it, listening to your favorite songs, going to a car dealership to look at the latest offerings, strolling through a museum or a tranquil place in nature, polishing a pair of shoes, organizing a cluttered space, or doing anything else that reminds you that you have control of your life. Ultimately, that's the lesson I learned from my father's absence. I am not and never was a victim and neither are you. It all starts with taking the first steps. It's up to you to decide the direction you want to go. I hope you enjoy your journey as much as I have mine.

ACKNOWLEDGMENTS

To Gary Brozek, thank you for your guidance and structure through this journey.

Erin Melon, Jennifer Rudolph Walsh, Bethany Dick, and the William Morris Agency, thank you for your representation and care.

Jonathan Tunick you have a great talent company, thank you for your representation.

Zachary Schisgal, you have amazing patience. We should figure out how to bottle it to share with the world, because the world could use it. Thank you for helping me through this process.

Thank you to everyone at Simon & Schuster for your thorough publishing care and great taste.

Jeff Frankel, friends through thick and thin. Thank you so much for your friendship through the years. Thank you to McKuin Frankel Whitehead LLP.

Bonnie DuBeck, thank you for being so wonderful to my family.

My dapper uncle, Jessie Fisher, I'm waiting to take you shopping on Rodeo Drive again.

My favorite cousin, Allan (Joey) Williams, and I don't care who knows it.

My wife and daughters, LaNette, Indigo, and Azure, "Let's watch a movie!" I love you guys.

Ian and Jan Teague, you lit the pathway to a better life through education for so many foster, underprivileged, and disadvantaged children over the years; God Bless you both.

The Teague Family Foundation.